D0834273

SCOTLAND WITH A STRANGER

NINYA

TEAL BUTTERFLY PRESS

PRAISE FOR SCOTLAND WITH A STRANGER

5 out of 5 Stars Your book club needs this book now!

This candid account of one woman's quest to find her mojo again is funny, touching, and sometimes a little alarming, but, above all, inspirational. A single mom with two teens, Ninya takes a leap of faith to meet up with an internet acquaintance, a self-proclaimed life coach, who says she has planned a tour of Scotland that will restore Ninya's soul. Once there, however, Ninya finds that, as the Buddha warned, no matter where you go, there you are. Alongside the vivid beauty of the Scottish wilds, Ninya rediscovers her strength and resiliency. The "life coach" turns out to, instead, be self-absorbed and the trip "plan" turns out to be more of a vague notion, but, in the confusion, Ninya finds the clarity she was missing: you have everything you need inside you, already.

5 out of 5 Stars Should be in the circle of Anne Lamott and Elizabeth Gilbert

I'd found it hard to concentrate on reading books during quarantine until this one! With two demanding children at home, I wasn't getting very far in any book that I picked up — until Scotland With A Stranger. I never put it down from start to finish. I completely tuned out the world so that this time when other things interrupted me, I was unaware, for example, that my name had been called several times before I heard it haha! I'd look up, mumble an answer, and get right back into the book. That's the best kind of reading and it'd been too long since I had that!!! Scotland With A Stranger was so honest and brave, it made me both laugh and cry, and was comparable to Anne Lamott! Memoirs and biographies have always been my favorite genre. This book is right there with Elizabeth Gilbert's Eat Pray Love!

5 out of 5 Stars Not Your Regular Memoir

You would think heading off to Scotland for 2 weeks with someone you have never met would fall under a serious mid-life crisis category. But for Ninya, it led to an amazing journey of self-discovery and forgiveness. Ninya has lived a roller-coaster of a life – dealing with more things than I can imagine. She lays it all out for us – the good, the bad, the ugly, the wicked. She is a real person, telling a real story. Completely unromanticized. Her writing style will have you feeling like you are right there with her, feeling all the feels. Bonus – not only does she describe the beautiful scenery but she has an online photo album available for you to see the pictures and videos she took. Ninya is an inspiration to women everywhere and a phenomenal author. I can't wait to read more from her.

5 out of 5 Stars Many Trips in One

Great, fast-paced read. Well-structured in alternating between the trip itself and the very personal events which built up to it. Plenty of humor (self-deprecating, my favorite kind), along with descriptions of Scotland that will inspire many future trips. Introspective without navel-gazing, and demonstrates journeys toward acceptance of self and peace with past disappointments. There's something here for everyone. I'll read this author again!

5 out of 5 Stars Not Just Another Memoir

There are things in life that speak to the deepest parts of our hearts; our triumphs, our failures, our hopes, our fears, our dreams, our pain.

For some it is art, for others, it is music.

For some, it will be this book.

Ninya shares, in an authentic and uncomplicated way, that she is living a life so many of us live.

The names are changed, the rooms are different colors, the smells vary in their complexity.

You will cheer her as she makes discoveries about life and self you yourself have made.

You will find hope in the lessons she has absorbed; lessons we all know intellectually, but may still be struggling to fully bring into ourselves.

You will want to hug away her pain, so much like your own.

You will want to assure her she is on a good path, she is worthy, she is strength.

She is another version of you, on paper for all to see.

She will remind you that your journey is YOUR journey, and yet it is the journey of us all.

And wherever that journey takes us, we are on a good path, we are worthy, we are strength.

5 out of 5 Stars Hard to Put Down

Start to finish, this book is well written! Finished in two readings because I wanted to see the story to it's conclusion. Ninya writes with raw emotion, humor, and puts to print those "inside" thoughts that so many of us keep inside. Her description of scenery and food makes me want to hop a plane today! This is a must read memoir!

5 out of 5 Stars A Memoir that Will Make You Look at Your Own Life Differently

Ninya's story defines bravery when facing mountains in one's life. Her memoir of taking a once-in-a-lifetime trip to Scotland with a virtual stranger will allow you to face your own stories of fear and betrayal and joy and success.

5 out of 5 Stars This is the Book We all Need

I bought "Scotland with a Stranger," as a signed copy, not really expecting much because, well, not everyone can be an engaging writer/author. I wanted to support my friend in her endeavors, though, in being a writer. Writing anything of a substantial, or entertaining, nature is hard and is an accomplishment I can never see for myself. So, when my copy came in the mail, I began with trepidation that my friend had quite possibly, and probably, missed her mark. This is the farthest from the truth – she nailed her goal with a sweet, just subtle, perfection that surely awes me.

The story follows Ninya from an addiction-laden marriage, to devastation from trying to parent a troubled teenage son, to other various hurdles in her life. There's a bit of bouncing back and forth between life pre-Scotland and Scotland, however, the storylines – the narrative – is easy to follow. She successfully links her past to her current, and in some instances, how the past has the ability to foreshadow her future. Life is about ups and downs of which Ninya seems to have had more downs than ups. Her story is relatable in a salient and relatable way. She shares with us, the reader, times in her life that are still very much taboo to talk openly about and we swim deeply into the past decade of her life like a whale in the ocean.

I was puzzled and perturbed while reading her story of going to Scotland with a stranger because the story seemed to revolve around her interactions with this stranger, Erika. The story is supposed to be about Ninya's journey to finding herself, right? Right?! I had to "sit" with the story for a day in order to see that Ninya discovered herself not through Scotland per se, but through her interactions with Erika. the inner monologue she had with Erika's antics. Scotland was the setting, however, like any great story, a well-defined protagonist (Ninya) and antagonist (Erika) are key. While I would have loved to have heard more about Scotland – the sights, the sounds, the smells – I think that it's just background, the experience of being some place new. As a social worker, I thought that Noah gave Ninya some really sound advice and insight though she may have chosen to ignore it in the beginning. Some of her more moving introspections were paring her personal experiences in Scotland's nature to remembering Noah's wise words.

I relate with Ninya. There were many times I cried while reading her feelings, her desperation. That utter need to "fix it," for everyone. That losing of oneself while doing for others. This read may very well prompt other readers to ask the questions, "Who am I?" and, "What do I like?" I recognized Ninya's resiliency much earlier than she. That resiliency is what allowed her to take on a journey in Scotland with a stranger. This journey is one that all women, especially all mothers, should take once in life. We need that pilgrimage to find ourselves again.

ALSO BY NINYA

Non-Fiction

Scotland with a Stranger: A Memoir

First You Then Him: A Former Trainwreck's Guide to Becoming
and then Finding a Healthy Partner

Erotic Romance

Velvet Guild Collection 1

Velvet Guild Collection 2

Velvet Guild Collection 3

Velvet Guild Collection 4

By Blair Bryan

(Ninya's Contemporary Fiction Pen Name)

Back to Before

Better than Before

The Sweetest Day

The Funologist

When Wren Came Out

AnaStasia Lived Two Lives

To My Children:

I loved you both from the first moment I knew you existed. Over the moon, all-consuming love. Nothing will ever change that.

I made so many mistakes. I pray you don't make the same ones.

And to Erin, Jessica, and Patrick—my team of three, who made this life-changing trip possible for me: I am forever grateful.

PREFACE

To write this book, I relied heavily on my private journals, blog posts, text messages, photographs, and videos. I recalled all the events and conversations from my memory as accurately as I could. All the names and identifying characteristics of the individuals portrayed have been changed to preserve anonymity. I omitted a few events leading up to and during the trip that had no impact on the substance of the story.

I have strived to tell this story as accurately and as truthfully as I can.

A FAIR WARNING

There are some pretty heavy topics in here, and a bit of profanity. If that offends you, then you will want to read something else.

CHECK OUT MY PHOTO JOURNAL
FROM THE TRIP

Photography is my other love.

Check out my photos from this life changing journey through Scotland at this link.

https://tealbutterflypress.com/blogs/travel-photography/scotland-may-2019-travel-photologue

ONE

Who goes to Scotland for two weeks with a stranger they met over the internet?

I did.

I remember the very first message; I was part of a women's photography group on Facebook, and I was nearing the end of my photography career. It was an uncertain time, and I was trying to figure out what was next for me professionally. This coated my life in fear that was nearly paralyzing, like a boat floating in the ocean, no longer tethered to the career that had been my identity. The last three years after my divorce had been punishing in nearly every measurable way, and I was completely depleted.

At the time, I was working exclusively from home, rarely leaving the house because, when I am depressed, I tend to hunker down and hide. I was sad and lost, and nothing seemed to make sense anymore, stuck in the soul sucking social media career I never wanted but which seemed to want me. The daily grind of it and the comparison factor left the sour taste of dissatisfaction in my mouth when I looked at the smoking wreckage of my life. Social media is the devil, camouflaged as connection. Showing us the greatest hits reels of people's lives, which we compare against our personal struggles, making us feel insignificant, unworthy, and less than. I was stuck in this land of fraud and make believe, unable to find an exit.

Every day was the same, stretched out before me, looking bleak and barren, and I just existed in the most basic ways, only fulfilling the basic needs for myself and my children. That day, I posted a photo in the group of the five-figure engagement ring I had just returned to the wrong man, needing some encouragement from strangers because my life was so isolating. And then I heard the Facebook messenger notification *ding,* and there it was. A message from a stranger named Erika.

I read your post. I have this idea I want to do. I know the mountains of Scotland. When I had to take my life back, I took off for Scotland and hiked and hiked and found myself again on the mountains. It was amazing.

I want to take a group of women there. Not like a workshop. But more just for self-healing. There is something special about Scotland. And don't worry, I know how to do it cheap.

I pray a lot, and when I was there last time, I knew I was supposed to do this.

I will just lead you. When I was there last time, I knew this was something I was called to do. I know the country. I know what you are going through, and I know the need to regain your sense of self. This is a God thing.

A God thing. The magic words. It hit my heart hard. I was raised Catholic, and it stuck, especially the guilt. I didn't identify as Catholic anymore, but I definitely believed in God, and nothing would ever change that. I have always had a wide-eyed optimistic 'Pollyanna' quality, always thinking things will get better, even when knee deep in disaster. I should have been a boxer. My ability to recover, knockout after knockout, was so strong, like one of those weighted superhero punching bags that take a pounding and then pop right back up again, over and over and over.

Hiking, healing, the trip of a lifetime… These words resonated in the deepest recesses of my heart. Being a self-help junkie since nearly birth, my library was filled with inspirational books, my favorites being those of journey and self-discovery stories like *"Wild"* and *"Eat Pray Love."* Those stories planted a seed in me that yearned for an experience like this, and the idea that I might *actually* have one in real life was thrilling.

It called to my soul in a way that there was nothing else I could say except yes. It just felt like it was the exact thing I needed, at the exact, right moment I needed it.

The messages flew back and forth furiously for a few minutes. Erika would plan everything. I would just need to show up and be transformed.

The people there are so happy.
Happiness and joy like you have never experienced before.
The landscape is so beautiful.
The mountains and waterfalls are amazing.
When I got to the summit, I cried.

Beauty. Joy. Happiness. I could use some of that. Those things had been so elusive for me for so long, I almost forgot they existed. She said we could do it all for less than $3000, so I made up my mind in seconds. I had been dying to use my passport since I got it a year and a half before. I had never been out of the country, ever, not even to Canada or Mexico, and I was ready! I was finally going to travel and do all the things I said I was going to do 'someday.' I was going to heal myself and reconnect with my soul on the mountaintops of Scotland. Finally, I was going to fill up my own well and figure out who I was now that I had no man in my life.

When I read her words through my cracked rose-colored glasses, I sobbed like a baby at the rightness of it all. When the student is ready, the teacher appears. I could not have been more excited and ready for an experience like this.

The next day, I wrote in my journal:

God sent me an angel in Erika. A guide, a leader, a sister. Someone who has been there. Who knows the struggle to get back to your sense of self when you have lost everything. When you don't know who you are anymore. When you are little and lost and broken. Someone who can gently guide you back to center. Who can push you to break through the sadness and pain to the other side. That is what Erika will do for me. I just know it.

Fair warning: I must also admit I have a flair for the dramatic and over romancing things in my head. Looking back now, I was a sitting duck. I mean, "God sent me an angel?" "When the student is ready, the teacher appears?" "Reconnect with my soul on the mountaintops of Scotland?" Reading those words now makes me want to puke in my mouth a little, but at the time, I was serious. It felt *so* right. It was *destiny*.

Yes, I am in. I am *all* in.

I needed this so badly.

That's how it started. A Facebook post in a group and a message from a stranger. That's all it takes to change your life.

TWO

How do you get to a place where you are open to trekking across a foreign country with a complete stranger to find yourself again? It's a lengthy and slow process. Once, in a sermon at my Catholic high school, Father Brunkan talked about how to cook a frog.

"You don't just throw a frog into a vat of boiling water. He'll fight you, desperate to jump right out. You put him in a nice bath of cool water. He loves it in there. It feels natural and good. And then you bring up the heat a little, and he thinks, 'Oooh! This warm water feels great!' And then you bring it up even more, and he says, 'Hmm, starting to get a little warm. I should probably get out soon. I will in a minute.' Then you crank it up even more until finally it's too late and he's cooked."

And that is how it happens. It's a series of settlings. It is wanting to be loved by someone, to be valued by someone so much that you are willing to compromise yourself. First, you are asked to do this in small ways, like overlooking how many drinks your boyfriend is drinking.

Your friends say, "He's a smoker. You said that was a deal breaker."

You counter that attack with, "No one is perfect. Everyone knows you won't find *everything* you are looking for in one person. You have to *compromise.*" And so, you do.

Years pass, and there are more settlings. There are the twelve bottles of vodka you find when you are cleaning out the garage one day. You confront him, and make him promise to get treatment, to go to the meetings, to get professional help. He says anything, makes any promise that needs to be made to keep you there. And so, you stay, because how can you leave a person at a time when they need you most? By the time you find the actual truth about the extent of the problem you are facing, you are pregnant. You do not want your baby to be without a father. He doesn't beat you. He doesn't emotionally abuse you. He has a *disease*. You wouldn't leave your partner if they had cancer, would you? Of course not. So you decide to stay and fight it together.

Then more years pass, and you are pregnant again. You find joy in the babies you are surrounded with. They are the light of your life and thriving under your dedicated and constant care, and you are *busy*. So busy. Thick in the constant neediness of motherhood. And you are *needed*. Oh! What a glorious feeling for someone like you. You live to serve others, you *need* to be needed, and no one is needier than an infant and a toddler, and an alcoholic.

Their lives consume yours, and taking care of your family while keeping your business running becomes your entire focus. He *lets* you do it all. Everything that needs to be done for kids, everything that needs to be done for him and the business. Keeping you constantly buried in the process of laundry, making meals, and disciplining children, so at the end of the night, you are exhausted and fall into bed clutching the baby monitor. While you sleep, he is free to sneak out of the house, to steal over to the bar to drink his many drinks, to sleep until the late morning, secure in the knowledge that you are there. You've got *it all* handled.

When you ask for help, he procrastinates and avoids your requests until you get frustrated and do it yourself. So, you stop asking him for help. You stop asking him for anything because you know it will just fall back on your shoulders anyway, so you might as well just do it in the first place and save your breath. This is where the bitterness sets in. This is where the anger, the frustration, and the martyr complex take root. You wear them as badges of honor and applaud yourself for being so selfless. So generous. So giving. You are incredible—a saint, really—and you begin to identify as Saint Ninya.

But then the children get older. They are more self-sufficient, giving you the luxury of more time. Numbed out during the last five years, you wake up one day with fresh eyes and find yourself nearing two hundred pounds on your five-foot-six-inch frame. A visit to the doctor confirms you are morbidly obese, so you engage yourself in the business of making changes and getting healthier. You exercise, start a healthy eating plan, and you lose weight. You start to feel stronger and more capable, and the kids get older, giving you even more time and energy to focus on the other things in your life that aren't working. But still, you are unable to see and unable to tackle the one that is the biggest monster in the room. You are married to an addict, and an addict will do whatever they need to do to continue their behavior.

You think a change of climate will help, so you busy yourself moving halfway across the country to Alabama. It's warm there; no more cold, snowy winters that you've grown to loathe. *Surely, I will be happy here*, you think. He agrees to the move, doing anything to keep you in a place where you will continue to take care of him. Because he doesn't know much, but he *does* know that he needs you to continue the caretaking. He needs you there to manage it all—the house, the business, and the kids. Without you, he would have to step up, and that is not something that interests him at all. That is something that will get in the way of all the lemon drops, without the lemon, that are his constant craving.

You think the change of location will transform your life, that you will finally be happy. But you are not. You are just overwhelmed. Exhausted again with the logistics of moving, of showing and selling a house you are living in with small children, of getting healthcare lined up in a new state when you are self-employed. You are consumed by finding customers in your new state, with getting the kids registered for school. Overloaded again and blind to the disease that is still feasting on your every effort. Endlessly ravenous, like a tapeworm consuming its host. Rendering your partner useless and actually turning him into someone *else* you need to take care of, someone you begin to hate.

Alabama is not the answer, so you return to your home state, with your tail between your legs. This time you are financially ruined, feeding your children ninety-nine cent boxes of pasta nearly every day and swallowing your pride to accept grocery deliveries from your father. Moving to Alabama was a huge gamble, and you lost. This revelation sends you spiraling into a deep depression that keeps you busy again, this time in your own mind. You still provide basic needs for the children and the helpless man you feel shackled to, but instead of enjoying life, you sit in fear and sadness. You wallow in pity and self-loathing. It is an endless cycle that is nearly impossible to break, and the long winter feels exactly like you feel, deep in the recesses of your soul. Desolate, bleak, and neverendingly cold.

Then, one day, your phone rings, and a voice you recognize instantly is on the other end, a voice you haven't heard in four years, asking for a meeting.

It is your mom. She needs to see you. It is important. You wonder, *why now?* But you go anyway, not knowing what to expect.

You hear the words 'Pancreatic Cancer.' You know this is a death sentence. Six weeks later, she is gone. GONE. And you are busy again. Busy with grief this time. Consumed with regret and lost time and the pain of being on the earth without your mother. Without your lifeline, without your anchor. You always thought, eventually, the problems with her would work themselves out, someday she would meet your daughter and someday she would choose to re-enter your life, and so you gave her space. But she never did, and now, she never *will*. The finality of this is devastating. It spins you out again, consuming all your resources to process, and so you still continue to take care of the lives that you created and the one you vowed to take care of in sickness and in health. You are spinning plates on the sticks, like the Chinese circus that came to town when you were a child. You run from plate to plate, spinning and spinning, desperate to keep anything from falling, and it takes every ounce of your life-force.

Then you turn forty, and all the clichés are true. At forty, the alarm is screaming. Until forty, you had successfully tuned it out. It was still going off, but you were able to ignore it for years, saying later. Later, I will do something. But now, it is nearly deafening, and you must act. So, you gather your meager resources, and you finally see for the first time, with fresh eyes, what the issue really is. Your marriage is a dysfunctional mess even years of therapy has never helped. You yearn to take care of your kids without the added burden of taking care of an adult addict. You want those resources you poured on him, resolving his problems, to be free to refocus on yourself. He will never change. That is obvious. You are done.

So, you ask for a divorce. A long, drawn out, messy divorce that takes almost two more of your precious years. Finally, you think things will get better. Now, you can all *heal*. But instead of healing, your kids are hurting. Because you hid all the problems in your marriage from them, because you didn't want to burden them, they had no idea the secret battles you were fighting. Their lives begin a freefall. They are searching for something to make them feel better. To make this crippling, newfound fear and anxiety go away. Your son reaches for drugs to do chase away his profound pain, and his descent into hell begins while all the battles are still being fought over the home and business. While you weren't paying close enough attention, he gets consumed by his need to escape the pain. When you finally see what is happening to your son, you react swiftly and strongly, getting him treatment and meetings. You send him away to a residential center because that is what the experts tell you to do and because you will do anything they say to make him healthy and happy. You want him to be *okay*. Your entire focus shifts to him, to what he needs—finding a good therapist, getting him on the right cocktail of drugs for his depression and anxiety. With whatever resources are left, you take care of the daughter who has been scarred by watching her family implode and her brother self-medicate.

The actions the experts recommend are not easy, and your son knows that all the big decisions and disciplinary consequences come directly from you because your husband never actively participated in the child-rearing. He was the fun dad and you were regulated to the judge and jury. You were *so* good at it that he left all the tough decisions to you. Because of this dynamic, your son doesn't trust you anymore. He sees you as the enemy. He runs away. He lashes out. He steals from you, and he lies. In tandem with his downward spiral, your daughter begins to suffer. Watching the entire unfolding of her brother's self-destruction is fundamentally changing who she is. It's destroying her, so you make the most difficult decision of your life when you decide to separate the kids. Since your son refuses to come to your home, to the only healthy place he could stay, you agree to let him live with his dad, who promises to give him a safe and sober place to live. Your ex-husband lies to your face, tells you he isn't drinking anymore and tells you he's attending daily AA meetings. So, you wrap your life around saving the child that you *can* save, feeling the enormous weight of shame and guilt that comes from choosing to save one child over the other.

Your entire existence is engulfed in outrage and anxiety. The kids are angry, your ex-husband is bitter, and you are terrified. Every unoccupied moment you punish yourself for the decisions you've made. Ruminating in shame and sadness where your life has led you, you wallow in a vast sea of self-hatred. To feel better, you seek out romantic relationships, but because you are unhealthy, the partners you find are toxic. The newness and dopamine keep you happy for a time. It takes your mind off of the constant pain you've been asked to endure, temporarily, but it always resurfaces, like a bobber you are trying to hold down under the water. Eventually, it rushes back to break the surface.

You are empty. You are lost. You are broken. You don't know how to do anything anymore, you don't trust yourself, and you don't think you are enough. This is the place you live, and when jetting off to Scotland becomes an option, this is why you need it. This is why you *must* go. This is why it speaks to you.

THREE

Even though my friends and family had a front row seat to the never-ending catastrophe that had been my life over the previous three years, it was still difficult to explain to my sister and my friends why I was going to Scotland with a stranger. Had I drunk too much of the new age Kool-Aid? This trip sounded slightly crazy, full of the woo-woo, and a little over dramatic. So, I kept most of my motivation to myself and in my journal:

God has seen me struggle. He has watched me make mistakes. He has whispered to Erika, "Here's your next assignment, and it's a doozy. She's really messed up." Erika is everything I want to be—strong, solid, happy, joyful, living on purpose.

I was catching up with one of my best friends one day. As we gobbled chips and salsa and sipped on margaritas, she gave it to me straight.

"You're doing what?" she asked.

"I'm going to Scotland."

"With who?"

"A life coach. I met her online in a women's photography group I'm in."

"But you don't *know* her."

"True, but we have mutual friends. If she was crazy, she wouldn't be allowed in the group."

"Wow, I would never be able to do that," my friend confided.

"I'm tired of waiting, of saying someday I'm gonna." The words were coming fast now. "I'm forty-three, someday needs to be now. She's been there several times, knows the area like the back of her hand, and knows where to go and where to stay so it's cheap. It's the adventure of a lifetime, and if I don't go now, I never will."

"Two weeks is a long time."

"She wanted to stay for three, but two is about all I can swing financially. I feel God brought her into my life to transform it," I gushed. "She says Scotland is magical and amazing. You can feel Jesus walking next to you, saying, 'You can do this.' Not rescuing you, but rather encouraging you to find the strength to do it yourself. She said that the healing continues even after you come home, that it completely changes you. Forever." I was all gooey eyed with love for Scotland already. The idea of it was so romantic and adventurous, which is what made it so alluring. I yearned for it.

"She is really opinionated," my friend continued. "I mean, the *stuff* she posts in your group. I don't think I'd last a week with someone like her. We'd probably kill each other."

I laughed because it was true. They would.

Erika was part of a secret group I had started on Facebook called Fun Chix. It was just a way for a group of like-minded females to blow off steam and laugh with other women at inappropriate things without them being public.

It's true, she *was* very opinionated, but that was one of the things that I initially admired about her. She was tough and outspoken. Deeply committed to taking care of *all* animals, especially horses, on her farm. She was a vocal Trump supporter and had been in the military. She was strong and tough and independent, all qualities I wished I had more of myself. We were truly polar opposites.

My friends were excited for me, and probably slightly shocked. I had never done anything like that before in my life, ever. Never impulsive, selfish, or thrill-seeking. I was a dutiful mother who self-sacrificed until it hurt. This was crazy and hard for them to understand because it was so out of character. I'm sure they thought, *Oh, Ninya's just having a midlife crisis.*

And they were probably right.

FOUR

I danced a little jig to the Skype ring signaling an incoming call. I had recently started healing therapy sessions with Noah in February before my trip in May. He lived in Florida, and our sessions involved a weekly Skype call while he worked on me over the internet. It was time for our second session.

His face popped up, and I smiled. Long brown ponytail, gentle spirit, soft smile. He radiated the calm peacefulness that I was desperate to find.

We settled into the call. Typically, I would talk about whatever was on my mind, and he would help me reframe it in a healthier way.

"I'm struggling, watching Liam decide to graduate a year early with no real plan. I wanted him to go to the community college, and his high school was going to pay the tuition for the first year. It would have given him something to build on. It's so hard to accept his decision to pass up this opportunity."

"You don't have to fix everything. It's not your role to fix him, and doing so takes away his power and ability to grow.

Stop fixing his stuff. Stop getting in the way. Let him take care of himself." His words were calm, his delivery steady. "You have to own your actions of going into someone else's life and weakening them by your need to be needed. Stop participating, and it will give you the strength to keep your resources for yourself."

It was true. I was a natural born fixer, and baby birds with broken wings were drawn to me. I attracted people in my life who needed me, my want to feel needed and worthy drawing them in. It was a sick pattern that I was desperate to change, but the funny thing was, it was a pattern I never fully acknowledged until I started working with Noah. I didn't own my own shit of needing to be needed; I preferred to take the martyr approach and proudly wear all this wonderful self-sacrifice as a badge of honor.

Look at what I have done for you.

"It's just so hard to see him make his life harder than it needs to be. And when we do communicate, it just becomes this battle of him lashing out and me trying to control."

"I can understand that. It's very hard to not fall back into that pattern," he continued, then paused. "Try this. Don't open the door, not through texting or through any other communication. Just keep the door closed. Use closed door statements like, 'I hope you can find the answer to that.' If you open your door, it just gets the dynamic going again and again. By keeping the door closed, it forces him to open his own door and fix himself."

"But what do I *say?*" I needed the exact words to say to stop myself from trying to fix him. A cheat sheet I could use to stop the destructive dynamic that had become the norm between us.

"I hope you find the answer you are looking for. That is all. Don't tell him he is screwing up, don't step up and try to fix it, don't hold space for it, and don't use any of your resources or emotions to fix his stuff."

"That will be really hard," I admitted.

"If you want the pattern to change, this is the only way it will."

We were both quiet for a moment, absorbing the information. Then I changed the subject.

"So, I'm going to Scotland in a month."

He smiled and looked closely at me through the screen. His silence was making me anxious. I'd never met anyone who was so thoughtful with his word selection. "That is amazing. Scotland is incredibly beautiful. Who are you going with?"

"Someone I met online. She is a life and fitness coach and wants to take women who have been through trauma to Scotland to heal."

He was quiet again for a really long time, making me uncomfortable. I heard the clock ticking on the table next to me. "I am worried for you, Ninya," he said quietly.

What did he know that I didn't? I laughed nervously and smiled trying to hide my growing anxiety.

"You attract people that take from you. You open your cupboard doors to them, and they take everything, and if there is even one crumb left, they come back and take that, too. They take all of your invisible resources."

Invisible resources? What in the what?

"Imagine a cupboard in your kitchen, the doors opened wide. You need to shut the doors and lock them for now until you become healthy enough to understand who it is okay to open them to."

"It will be fine," I asserted, trying to brush off his concern. "She's a friend of a friend. I mean, she's not a *total* stranger." I responded, trying to reason my way out of his worry. That was a lie I was telling myself. We had mutual acquaintances, but she *was* a total stranger.

He was quiet and accepted that explanation. "Okay. I hope that it is, and I hope you get a chance to reset. You need to ground yourself as much as possible."

"What do you mean?"

"The earth has the ability to calm and balance your hormones. Take off your shoes and go barefoot as much as possible when you are in a place where you can do that."

"I definitely will."

"Much strength to you, Ninya. We will talk next week."

Noah was a wise man, brought into my life by a cousin by marriage. I was stuck in all the ways, and my own anxiety and depression were reaching a fevered pitch. Lost in myself, I had to take care of my daughter and co-parent my son with an alcoholic. It had worn me down to nothing. There was nothing left for me, and I knew I couldn't continue this way. Something had to change, and Scotland was going to change it.

FIVE

The catalyst for the trip in the first place happened sixteen months before Scotland, when I ended my engagement to a man I had been with for nearly two years. It was hard to walk away from someone who loved me in his way, but in the back of my mind, I always knew it wasn't right. I hemmed and hawed over it for months before finally gathering up the courage to end it. In a state of constant turmoil, my body was sending signals that something was wrong, with shooting pains, tingling, and numbness down my neck and arms. I was in a state of constant anxiety. Sleep eluded me like never before. It was the physical manifestation of my emotional health. I stayed in the relationship longer than I should have because it wasn't just about me and what *I* wanted. It was also about three children who didn't deserve any more pain.

His son, Jack, and my son, Liam, were both fifteen. Jack was sweet and loving, a talented athlete, and easy going. I was going to be his bonus mom, and I loved him deeply. We bonded over simple things like taking Jack to dentist appointments and sending his dad funny videos of him trying to talk with a mouthful of Novocain. I enjoyed teaching him how to cook since he was always willing to help out in the kitchen.

Liam was always the clown, willing to embarrass himself to make everyone laugh. One day, he somehow stretched a condom over his head like a hat, pulling it down over his eyes and nose. It smashed his features together, forming a pig nose, which was hysterical on its own, but he took it one step further and proceeded to blow it up using only his nose. It was literally ten inches tall and around his entire head, the tip becoming the weird rounded point of a plastic see-through hat. I didn't even know latex could do that. Then he ran around the house, calling himself King Condom. Liam was one of the funniest and wittiest people I'd ever met, a gift he inherited from my Dad.

Josie was twelve and artistic. She had real gifts for drawing, creating digital art, making music, and applying makeup. When God made her, he accidentally tripped with the creativity jar in his hands (which, in my mind, looks a lot like a huge pot of glitter) and dumped the *entire* contents on her. He patted it down and swirled it around, trying to distribute it evenly—like when a two-year-old accidentally dumps four teaspoons of colored sugar on one cookie—and said, "Well, this should be interesting. Let's see how this one turns out." In the long run, my indecision ended up hurting everyone more, especially the kids. Indecision paralyzed me, and that is why I stayed; I needed to be absolutely sure. I didn't want to hurt them unless there was no other way. I needed to be certain.

I have always been an obsessive journalist. In those pages, I knew months before what the right decision was, but I couldn't bring myself to carry it out. So, I stayed stuck in anxiety and indecision. Looking back now, the pain could have been avoided by being true to myself. I just didn't know how to trust myself anymore. Eventually, I couldn't ignore the call of my heart, and on the day I steeled my resolve to actually break the engagement, I wrote:

Today, I have to give back a beautiful ring to a decent human being. It's not because I'm right or he's right; it's because we are wrong for each other. He will be angry, I am sure. He will be confused and not understand. Dig at me and try to generally make himself feel better by hurting me. I am ready for that. I am ready to move forward with my plan. To line up the mover and get things sorted. Start packing things in boxes yet again. Fresh start number three in two years.

I glanced down at the ring, heavy on my hand, turning it around and around on my finger, and then I took it off and looked down at my hand again. Somehow, I thought one way would feel more right, and the true path I should take would be revealed by the way I felt when I looked down at my left hand. I felt nothing either way, except the constant gnawing. It was an interior struggle that consumed my daily resources and made it hard to focus on anything else.

I yearned for simplicity. For minimalism. For doing what I needed to do for the next two years to ensure my kids could stay in their schools and graduate.

In the journal, I continued:

I will work on myself and lick my wounds and try to figure out what the fuck happened and how I continue to settle for things. Relationships that aren't partnerships. Work that doesn't make me feel like my best self. There is a great big

world out there, and I want to explore it. I want to be coura-
geous in all aspects of my life. I want to listen to my own
heart for a while. To learn to trust myself and understand
who I am and what I bring to the table. I want to learn to love
myself so I can move forward in life and feel worthy and
enough just as I am.

I took a photo of the ring. I have always been an obsessive photo taker, painstakingly recording moments and memories since I was a child. Sentimental to the core, partly because trauma changes the way your brain stores memories, I always wanted to cling to them, especially the happy ones since, in recent years, they had been so few.

It was easily the most beautiful piece of jewelry I would *ever* own. But when it comes attached to a life you don't want to live, the beauty diminishes. It was becoming a tiny handcuff, chaining me to a reality that everything inside me knew was wrong.

I searched for the words, the right words to say to break a man's heart in the gentlest way possible. A man I had promised to marry. My stomach rolled, and the anxiety was fueling everything. Most of my mornings were spent looking out of the window of the beautiful kitchen of the house that Cal had bought for our blended family's life to begin. Watching the birds fly, and the progress on the homes being built behind us, I wished I could fly away from the mess I had made.

He had recently developed a habit of coming home and going directly to the basement. It was his safe place, I think, away from the stress and worry of raising nearly three teenagers who lived to press our buttons and the boundaries as far and as fast as they could.

The kids weren't home yet, so this was the best time to

give him the news. I knew he would be angry, and I didn't want to expose them to it, knowing the mess was completely my fault.

Tell him straight, then give him the ring and leave.

My hands shook as I took the ring off for the final time and tucked it into the pocket of my coat. I gathered up my purse and my keys, not wanting to stay after delivering the news, knowing he would try to plead and persuade me. Knowing that nothing was going to change my mind.

I walked down the stairs and found him at the bottom.

"What's up?" He looked at me.

"This isn't working. We need to untangle our lives."

"What do you mean?" He moved closer, filling up the space between us.

"I made a decision to get an apartment, and I think I need to give you this back."

"You have got to be kidding me," he murmured.

I pulled the ring out of my pocket and placed it in his hand.

"Do you want me to find somewhere else for me and the kids to sleep tonight?"

He shook his head no, then I could feel the switch flip and knew the anger was coming next. "Maybe whatever guy you've been lining up next has some room at his place," he snarled. He was incredibly intelligent, his words always his favorite weapons. "You can't be alone, Ninya. There is always someone else."

"There's no one else, Cal." And it was true. There wasn't.

"You'll never be happy." He lashed out again. I didn't blame him, and part of me even wondered if he was right.

He turned the ring over and over in his hand. "Wow. Getting a symbol of your love and commitment handed back to you. That's rough."

"I wanted a future with the man on the bridge, Cal. That

is not who you are." The bridge was a special place for us, where he was gentle and kind and held me and whispered about our future. "I am going to focus on myself and my kids for now and get out of this depression."

Still in attack mode, he shot back, "Your kid ruined our relationship, plain and simple, so don't point your judgmental finger at me."

There was some truth to that statement, but it stung. It wasn't entirely my son's fault, but the chain of events from his bad decisions had taken a serious toll on everyone.

His voice was getting louder, his words sharper. "I'm still getting over the crap from the summer and fall, and from the constant threat of losing you. I never get to feel settled or at peace, ever. Every fucking two weeks, you're on my ass, threatening to leave and telling me I haven't changed. How the fuck am I supposed to change when I'm constantly under the gun with you?"

His neck was becoming red and blotchy, the telltale sign of his anger crawling up the sides of his cheeks. I knew him well enough to know it was a stress reaction. I watched the red fight to dominate his face, saying nothing, not wanting to provoke him further.

"This is bullshit, but it doesn't fucking matter now. Change takes time. We are barely out of the fucking fire, and your impatient ass just wants to bolt. I have to wonder if drama is something you can't live without."

I was starting to wonder the exact same thing. In fact, my previous therapist and I had a discussion about how I would need to learn to live with the boredom and emotional flatness and not create drama to fill it, just because that felt normal to me.

He was hurt, and so I just listened. He was always vocal when we fought, so I stayed there, quietly listening to him lash out. It was my penance for destroying his life, and I thought I deserved to hear the consequences of my actions.

"The fog is finally starting to lift off me, and you jump ship. I'm just gonna take these as signs as it's not meant to be because I cannot win for shit with you! All I hear is, 'You aren't the same.' Well, news flash, neither are you. You are dull and dusty. You haven't been the same person for a long time, and you are *far* from the person I fell in love with. The difference is I know why, and I'm not shoving it up your ass every couple of weeks. I'm not the same, but neither are you, so fuck you, Ninya."

He used to call me his bright and shiny. Dull and dusty was definitely more accurate now, but it hurt just the same. I was a shell of what I once was. I never really got to figure out who I was or what I needed because I distracted myself with back-to-back relationships after my divorce, and then I couldn't figure out what I needed inside of them.

He was quiet then, looking at the ring in his hand. I turned and walked up the stairs quietly and let myself out, shutting the door to the basement. Instantly, I knew it was the right decision because I felt lighter, free. I hated I had to hurt someone who loved me, and I hated I wasn't strong enough to realize earlier that the relationship wasn't the right one. I was sad I wasn't going to be a bonus mother to his son, who I had gotten close to over the last two years. Steeling myself for the kids' reactions to yet another move, the third in two years, I knew for the first time in maybe forever that I had to choose me. Because at the end of the day, that is all I really had.

SIX

A week later, it was official, and a plan was made.

"You're making a mistake. You'll be back." He was angry and shoved a Bundt cake pan at me, but I couldn't make eye contact. The Christmas tree was still up, now a few weeks into January, but the cheer was completely gone. It was another reminder of the dead relationship we were stuck in.

I packed up the kitchen silverware I was allotted, while Frank, our sweet little wiener dog, nipped at my feet. This part was painful. He insisted on going through everything together, piece by piece, partly because he was trying to spend time with me in the hopes that I would change my mind, but mostly because he didn't trust me. He trusted me more than he had ever trusted any other person in his life, but the fresh betrayal of that trust cut back all the new growth completely and stunted him again. It was an agonizing sorting process, and I left much behind, knowing that cookie sheets and pressure washers could eventually be replaced.

Cal lobbed another one at me. "Women love me. It will be easy to find a new you."

I let that slide, knowing he was over compensating, trying to make himself feel better about what was happening.

I also let slide the gym selfies he was posting daily on his Facebook page, as well as his change in relationship status from engaged to in a relationship. It was very telling that I didn't even wonder or care who this "new relationship" was with. He was trying to get a reaction out of me, and I didn't give him the pleasure of knowing that it hurt.

"You'll be back in a week. I know what's out there," he speculated.

"Oh, so you've switched to men now?" I joked, trying to lighten the mood, unable to resist.

He laughed and continued, "No, I just remember what the women I went on dates with used to say. I can go out with a new one every night if I want. Women eat me up. I won't be on the market long."

"Then you should," I agreed quietly. His ego was huge, it still is. Mostly a defense mechanism born from a childhood of not feeling good enough. I understood it, but it still annoyed me.

The kids were like ghosts, staying in their rooms, staggering their meal times. I relied on the crock pot, so we didn't have to see each other if we didn't want to. It was painfully quiet, and I tried to make it as easy as possible for everyone.

"The mover will be here at noon on Monday."

"So, I guess this is really happening," he finally admitted. This was very surprising to hear since I was literally packing up my possessions in boxes in front of him, but this was the statement that made it seem real. He walked to the couch and turned on the TV pulling the hood of his hoodie up. It had always been his security blanket. Frank settled into his neck area, knowing his job was to comfort at least one of us.

"Yes, it is."

"You know this is bullshit." He sighed. So many sighs from him lately. "We belong together."

I said nothing. Disagreeing would only lead to another lengthy, exhausting rehash of everything that had happened over the last two years. My mind was becoming freer. I didn't want to continue a painful post mortem of the relationship. I just wanted it to be over.

We still slept in the same bed, lying silently next to each other without touching. Except for the last night—the last night, we turned toward each other.

"You are being impulsive. You are making a mistake. I was just starting to feel better," he pleaded, trying to convince me to stay.

I hugged him tightly, burying my face in his chest.

He doesn't understand that these worries have been in my head since July. Seeing our lives unravel and the stress it caused. My anxiety about him and my kids. Co-parenting when we had vastly different styles was impossible. It just doesn't work.

He kissed me then, and our bodies said goodbye to each other in the quiet way we had become accustomed to that always left me wanting a little more from him. More kisses and more touches, more affection. He called me a bottomless pit and hated my neediness, making me feel like there was something wrong with me. Maybe, that last night, he was right. Maybe, that last night, it *was* neediness that made me turn toward him to feel better, even if it was just for a moment, to comfort him and to comfort myself.

The next morning, he left for a work trip. He kissed me goodbye and said, "Get your shit straightened out. Don't fuck up another man's life like you did mine."

SEVEN

Two months before Scotland, I lost half of my income. I was doing some social media consulting with a photographer and inventor, and it had been going well, but then he had a major life change and decided to go in a completely different direction. My position was eliminated. The extra money had given me a cushion. It had allowed me to take my daughter to the theater, one of the things we had always loved to do together. I had a budget to travel finally— a New Orleans trip with girlfriends, a trip to Virginia Beach to see my Dad, and then, of course, Scotland.

For the last sixteen years, I had been working with my ex-husband in the business we created, teaching photography online. My ex is an incredible photographic artist, and so we built the business around his art and teaching abilities. In that role, I spent a lot of time on social media, but I also produced educational content for his students. After the divorce, it became increasingly difficult to continue the business together, and I was trying to find a way out of it. It wasn't healthy for either of us to continue working together when so much had been destroyed. For a long time after our divorce, we were able to keep things together because I was very good at my job, but the level of distrust and disrespect was like a cancer eating away at the business. It was obvious that something permanent needed to change.

For sixteen years, I built my life on quicksand, working and building a beautiful home and business as hard and as fast as I could, but addiction undermined my every turn. It washed out the foundation that was so full of cracks, it was inevitable, but still, I clung to this false sense of security out of fear.

After the divorce was final, I began working on creating my own educational website for iPhone-ography. I was working nearly 24/7 to find a way to stand on my own two feet, so I was dependent on no one. I had started the site two years prior, but it was proving impossible to find traction. Coupled with the fact technology and apps were constantly changing, made the topic that much more difficult. The courses I created became obsolete in mere months. It was a project that crashed and burned and that I was still struggling to make successful when it was time to go to Scotland. I was getting angry and bitter I could always seem to find success for others, but never for myself. I was always a background player, pushing others to greatness, but every time I tried to stand in the spotlight, the light instantly shut off. It was an incredibly frustrating process that constantly left me scrambling for security and kept me weak and desperate.

In the months leading up to Scotland, I was searching for authenticity. I was deeply depressed and turning to podcasts and books to help change my mindset. The struggle had been all too real for far too long, and I still hadn't found my place in the world. The podcasts encouraged me to be true to who I was, to go all in on myself, to find my own truth and to live it out, and a huge unknown part of that process was finally finding what I was put here to do. When I look back at it now, it was always so simple. I can't believe it took me forty-three years to see it. Writing was always my one true thing. It was something I have done since I was little. I vividly remember lying on a quilt covered bunk bed with a notebook in hand, writing little stories, happy as a clam. Since then, I have journaled nearly daily and even attempted to write a book in my twenties, which now lives in the slush pile. A book so terrible it should never see the light of day. For some reason, I was blind to the idea of being a professional writer. I never identified as a writer; it was just something I did in the mornings to make sense of my life.

When I started dating Ryan, I finally gave myself permission to be a writer. On one of our first dates, the kind of date where you are telling each other your stories, he said after hearing a few of mine, "Wow. You need to write those down. You're a writer."

It was like the angels started singing, and the world all made sense for a second. You know how you know the truth when you hear it? I finally knew it. I was a writer.

The next day, I changed my Facebook handle to @NINYAauthor, I changed my Instagram Tagline to Ninya the writer, and I was out of the closet, loud and proud. I'm sure my friends and family had another bit of an eye roll at the news. *Here Ninya goes again. What is this, her fourth new business in three years? Now she's a writer, at least for the next couple of months.*

In preparation for Scotland, I ordered a keyboard for my iPad so I could travel lighter. I could write anywhere inspiration struck, and how could it not strike in Scotland? I was going to get a taste of every aspiring author's dream lifestyle —alone with my laptop, writing in a beautiful foreign country. I had no idea how addictive that first taste would be.

Losing my second income was a blow that came with a silver lining. I had an influx of time to pursue what I was being called to do. I had permission to call myself a writer, and I was finally ready to work toward my dream, but all the extras were gone—theater tickets, travel experiences, Botox, and prescription-grade skin care. All the things I had spoiled and distracted myself with disappeared. I adjusted my lifestyle significantly and briefly thought about not going to Scotland, but I had already paid for most of it. Out of pocket, it was only going to be around $1500 while I was there. This trip was the chance of a lifetime, and I was willing to go into the hole a bit to have it.

This is the worst possible time for me to go. But maybe that is exactly why I should.

EIGHT

At the end of March, I was scrolling Facebook in the very early morning during my job as a social media manager and group administrator, when a news story caught my eye.

"Budget Airline Wow Air Collapses and Cancels all Flights, Stranding Passengers." Wow Air registered in my usually foggy brain.

Wasn't that the airline that Erika was using to fly to Scotland?

She had scored me decent airfare on United, and I had booked my ticket, but I was almost certain she found the lowest rates for herself on Wow and booked it several months prior. A tiny knot formed in my stomach, and I was anxious to talk to Erika since our flight was scheduled in less than six weeks.

Since it was four a.m., I distracted myself with work, waiting for it to be a decent hour to call Erika. I waited until I saw the green dot pop up next to her name on Facebook messenger and immediately sent her a message.

Me: Did you see that Wow Air canceled all flights?

Erika: What? No way! You're kidding me!

I sent her a link to the article. She hadn't heard it and immediately panicked. So, did I.

Erika: I need to call my bank. I need to talk to my husband. I'll call you back.
Me: Just call your credit card company and they'll refund it. You really need to book a ticket today. I mean, it's only six weeks away.
Erika: I don't have a credit card. I used a debit card to book it. I'll call you back.

No credit card? How do people live like that? How did she travel in the past?

The adventure of my life was crumbling before my eyes. I couldn't go by myself. I was terrified at the prospect of international travel, being completely alone in a country I didn't know at all. I had booked a non-refundable ticket, had waived the insurance, and had gotten all my gear. The over-priced hiking shoes and backpack were waiting in my closet, but Scotland was getting further and further away. I was going to have to put this on hold like everything else I had done in my life. Make a plan, then set it aside for later. *It is not your turn. You will need to wait.* Become more frustrated and bitter. It was a recipe I knew well.

The phone rang, and it was Erika, her voice happier.

"My bank is awesome. They are going to refund my money, but it will take several business days," she said. "I'm so relieved."

"You need to book something now," I insisted, fully panicking that she wouldn't be able to find a ticket with all the displaced people from Wow Airline now in the mix.

"I can't. I need to wait until I get the money back in my account."

How long will that be? And will there even be any tickets left? Will I be living inside of the Edinburgh airport, waiting for her? Visions of that Tom Hanks movie where he lives in the airport started to fill my mind. Washing my socks in the airport sink and living off overpriced wilted salads did not sound very therapeutic.

"Just put it on my credit card and pay me back before the bill comes," I offered, making a split decision. Even though it wasn't ideal, I *needed* to know she was flying in to meet me, and buying the ticket gave me peace of mind.

"Really?" she asked, shocked.

"Yes, it's not that big of a deal as long as you pay me before the bill is due."

"I really appreciate this. I'll pay you back. I'm good for the money," she said.

I thought about her beautiful home and acreage and the several horses she owned and took care of, photos of the amazing greenhouse and kitchen she posted on Facebook. She seemed to be doing well, so it didn't seem like a risk at all.

"I found a ticket," she announced a few minutes later.

I gave her my credit card number, and she bought it and told me to download the Venmo app so she could repay me.

How does an adult human function without a credit card? Especially someone who travels overseas?

Those should have been red flags or, at the very least, some orange ones. But I had just spent a lifetime ignoring red flags. They had become nearly impossible for me to see. In hindsight, I should have asked more questions, but I was naive and trusting.

It took her nearly a month to pay me back, and that was only a partial payment, with the promise to pay the rest in a week or two.

That should have been another red flag. But it wasn't.

She finally paid me in full a few weeks before departure, but she did. So, everything was okay, right?

Wrong. So wrong.

NINE

In mid-April, a month before my flight, prom night arrived. My son was graduating an entire year early, so this was going to be the only prom night of his life. While in residential treatment, he was diagnosed with ADHD and finally properly medicated. Being prescribed Adderall was life-changing for him. For the first time, he could focus, and he had nothing but time on his hands. So, while in treatment, he powered through over twenty credits that all transferred when he completed his stay there. Since he was so far ahead, his big desire was to be finished with high school. He was so young, so impulsive, and I wanted him to take the free year of college credit he could have gotten instead of graduating early, but he refused. His mind was made up, and he was done.

The events of the summer before combined with the hard decisions I made fueled his anger, coloring every interaction we had. He didn't trust me at all. He hated my rules and my control, especially after living at his dad's house for the last several months, choosing the easy way out. There he was allowed to do things that I would never allow, where the rules were soft and never enforced.

I am a sucker for these big moments with my kids, a sentimental photo freak that cries at the drop of a hat. This was my one chance to have that moment, to see him dressed up and happy and enjoying life. A few weeks prior, we picked out a tux and a navy bowtie to match his girlfriend's dress, and he was happy, enjoying the idea of dressing up in a tux. It was strange to see him being fitted for formal wear. Your mommy mind starts the playback of memories right there in the tuxedo shop, from the day he was born when I saw the cleft in his chin for the first time, to the little boy that would ride his tricycle around the square while I sang a modified version of "Mustang Sally" that included his name. The days are long, but the years are short—that phrase is truer than I ever imagined. My only request was that I got to take pictures of him and his date, which he promised I could and said he would let me know where and when.

On the day of prom, my texts went unanswered most of the day. I finally got a response from his girlfriend with the details and showed up at Centennial Park ten minutes before they were due to arrive. I had my camera ready and couldn't wait to see him. I was already sad and feeling left out since I wanted to see him get dressed, to tie his tie, and to pick the imaginary lint off his jacket. I wanted to show him how to attach cuff links. I wanted to have that moment, that memory, but he wouldn't allow it. And so, I gave him space.

They were late pulling up, and he was instantly annoyed. He was anxious and stressed, and his face was pinched as he stepped out of the car.

"Oh, honey, you look so handsome," I said, forcing a hug on him. His tie was loose, and I tried to tighten it, but he was frustrated and pushed my hands away. He needed a haircut, and his pants were too short. He pulled them down to conceal the ankle monitor.

A few adults formed a circle that I joined. "Hi, I'm Liam's mom. You must be Nicole's parents." I stuck my hand out, and they shook it, but I could see and feel their disgust. I felt dirty, like I was something they had scraped from the bottom of their shoe. They hated that their daughter was dating my son.

Liam was sick, coughing and sneezing. I had brought a bottle of cough syrup with codeine with me and gave him a spoonful, hoping it would be enough to give him some relief so he could at least enjoy the dance. I never realized I'd have some explaining to do when his probation officer called me the very next day when he failed a random drug test.

I busied myself taking photos of Liam and his date on the bridge. He rolled his eyes and smiled on command. It was the fake one, but I snapped away anyway, knowing this was the best I could hope for.

I stepped backwards with the camera held to my eye, trying to get a full-length photo of them, and then felt fabric tugging behind me. I looked over my shoulder.

My dirty tennis shoe was on the hem of a white dress of one of Liam's friends.

"Oh my God, I am so sorry." Horrified, I apologized over and over. My face was red hot with embarrassment.

Liam watched this interaction, embarrassed.

"Are you done yet?" he asked, irritated.

I was frustrated with his dismissive tone but trying to be accommodating. "Can you take a photo of us?" I handed the camera to Nicole, and she snapped a photo of us.

Liam was coughing, keyed up, looking uncomfortable, and annoyed.

"Just go, Mom," he demanded.

Dismissed. Just like that. But I pushed the hurt and the

anger down because I didn't want to fight or be responsible for ruining his evening.

"Have a great time tonight, honey. Make some memories," I rattled on, forcing the excitement into my voice and the smile on my face. I wanted to hug him but was afraid of the possibility of rejection, so I walked to the Jeep defeated, looking down.

He sent me away. The other parents were allowed to stay, to take photos, to savor that moment. I pulled away with tears in my eyes, watching parents hug their sons one last time. I had wanted prom to be the happiest day of his high school career. He was going to graduate a few days after I got back from Scotland. There weren't many more opportunities to make memories as a teenager, and I just wanted him to have this one night where he was a normal, happy, healthy teenager doing things that teenagers were supposed to do.

I was crushed. It was a slap in the face, a report card on my mothering. He couldn't stand to be around me and was embarrassed I was even there. It was supposed to be this amazing memory, this moment in time that the sentimental part of me lived for. I drove to Ryan's and drank three margaritas, one after the other, to dull the pain. I sobbed, scrolling through Facebook, seeing all the prom posts and the proud parents posing with their kids in formal wear. I was so jealous, and I wanted that moment so much. It was devastating that I never got it.

I heard Noah's voice in my head.

You need to feel this. You need to grieve the relationship you wanted and thought you would have, and then accept what is.

I cried and cried and cried.

The next morning, a text from my daughter, Josie, lit up my phone.

Josie: Mom, I need you to come get me.

And another one quickly.

Josie: Now. I want to come home. Now.

My daughter hadn't seen her dad in a long time, and this was the first overnight visit in several months. I was trying to mentally prepare her for the nearly two weeks she was going to be spending with him while I was in Scotland. Her dad promised she would be safe there, told me of the AA meetings he was going to with Liam. Things were good, he was sober, and he could handle it.

She ran out of the house as soon as I pulled into the driveway. It was obvious she had been waiting by the window.

Visibly upset, her eyes red, she jumped in and slammed the door to the Jeep.

"What happened?" I could feel the anger tightly coiled in her thin frame.

"Dad has a new roommate, and so he had me sleep in his bedroom."

"Yeah," I replied, scared about what was going to come next.

"I felt something in the bed."

The panic was rising.

"There was a gun in the bed, Mom." She looked at me, her green eyes huge. "A gun!"

What. In. The. Fuck? I willed myself to stay silent, waiting for the rest of the story.

"I yelled for Dad, and when he came in, he said that it was there for my protection. If anyone came through the door, I should just shoot them."

Rage surfaced. White hot anger. I was stunned, speechless for nearly a full minute.

"So, what did you do?" I asked, forcing a calmness into my voice that I did not feel.

"I picked up the gun, put it on the nightstand, and then tried to go back to sleep. But he kept coming in the room every hour, waking me up, asking me if I needed anything."

Unbelievable. Sober my ass! Drunk Bastard. I will kill him.

"I don't feel comfortable there."

"Of course, you don't. That is not okay. You are never going back there." I drove quickly home, tailgating and taking turns fast, and when we got to the apartment, I sent Josie up to let the dog out and punched the numbers into my phone fast and hard.

He picked up on the first ring, which was unusual for him since he normally ducked my calls every chance he got.

"What in the fuck, Toby?"

"Please don't talk to me like that, Ninya, or I will end this phone call."

"You haven't seen your daughter in months, and she tells me you have her sleep in a bed with a gun in it?" I was trying to keep my voice under control, but it was getting louder with each word.

"It was for her protection."

"Was...it...loaded?" I asked, clearly enunciating each syllable.

"Well, duh. You can't protect yourself with an unloaded gun," he answered matter-of-fact, like it was the most logical statement in the entire world.

"Let me make sure I got this correctly. You had our fourteen-year-old daughter sleep in a bed—with a loaded gun? What were you thinking?" The sentences came out slowly and loudly and with such complete rage-fueled-control that each word was practically its own sentence. My voice grew even louder and pitchy, and my whole body was shaking. I felt nauseous.

"I guess I never thought about it like that."

"You never think! You *never* fucking think!" I shook my head in disbelief and shock. "I thought we agreed that all your guns would be stored in the safe at all times."

"You don't get to decide how I choose to protect my home. We aren't married anymore."

"I *do* if our fucking fourteen-year-old daughter is in your care!" It was loud and filled up the Jeep. I just couldn't hold back anymore.

"I'm hanging up now. I am not going to talk to you when you act like this."

The dial tone sounded in my ears.

I slammed my hands on the steering wheel and screamed a string of obscenities that would make a sailor blush. I yelled and cried and beat my hands against the wheel until they were red. I could feel my heartbeat in my head. I hated him. I hated that I could never count on him. I hated that I could never trust him. I hated that he was damaging our children with his insane thinking. I hated that he wasn't a parent and that I had chained myself to him for nearly twenty years. I hated myself for ever thinking this man was enough, for setting my standards so low that he was my choice for the father of my children. I hated him. I hated myself.

TEN

After that insane overnight visit, and with less than four weeks before I was due to leave, it was obvious I couldn't leave my daughter with my ex-husband. She wasn't safe there, and I would be consumed with worry during a trip I was taking to heal myself. It would have rendered the trip useless. School was in session, so I couldn't send her to my sister, who lived two hours away. My close friends couldn't take her. It was a lot to ask someone to take your teenage daughter for two weeks. She couldn't drive, but she also worked and had extra-curricular activities. My dream of Scotland was drifting farther and farther away.

I was walking on the trails and dialed my boyfriend.

"I don't think this trip was meant to happen. First, the airline closed, and now I can't find a place for Josie to stay for two weeks. I've asked everyone."

We'd only been together for six months, and he lived thirty minutes from me and worked another thirty minutes farther away, making the trip from his work to my house an hour. Not to mention, he didn't have kids, let alone experience with a teenager. It was a lot to ask him to take on when things were still relatively new.

"What about Megan and Emily?" he suggested. They were new friends that I met when I moved to Waukee, but we weren't at that place yet. I felt it was too much to ask at that point in the friendship.

I walked and stewed until I finally got the courage to ask him. "I know it's a lot to ask, but do you think you could do it for me?"

He hesitated. "You need to go, and I am willing to do whatever I can to make that happen. But try to reach out to Megan and Emily and see if they can help a few days during the week, and then we could probably make it work."

I hung up the phone and texted our group chat.

Girls, I am desperate. Josie can't stay with her dad. Something happened and it's not safe. I leave in 24 days and have nowhere for her to go.

Immediately they both responded.

We've got this.
Absolutely.
No problem, we will work it out.

A few weeks later, Ryan made a calendar and sent it to everyone. Emily took it a step further and color coded it, put Josie's work shifts in it, and coordinated times with pick-ups and drop-offs. In just a few days, a master calendar was set up, without me having to stew and worry about it. Ryan, Emily, and Megan stepped up to help me in the most selfless and beautiful way.

I was going to get to go to Scotland after all. And the best part was, instead of worrying the entire time about what was happening to Josie at her dad's house, she would be cared for by healthy people who knew how to handle the responsibility. She was going to stay with Megan's family and with Ryan on the weekends. Emily and her mother were going to make sure she got to work and school. I couldn't believe that this group was stepping up to help me, but I was so grateful for their support. The heaviest weight had been removed from my shoulders. I could go to Scotland and completely focus on what I was going there to do. It was a gift.

ELEVEN

The Skype ring played again. It was my final session with Noah before leaving for my trip to Scotland.

"You have been on my mind, Ninya. How have you been?" Noah radiated goodness. I had never been in such a presence of kind, positive energy like that before.

"I'm good. Scotland is soon, so I am wrapping up things to go there."

"That will be incredible for you. It's a beautiful place."

"I was hoping you could give me some guidance on what to do or things to focus on while I am away."

He closed his eyes and did this thing where he breathes and puts his fingers to his temple and then exhales loud and says profound things. When he did this the first time, I was so uncomfortable that I searched for words to say to fill the awkwardness. Now, I was learning to just breathe and be quiet, that the silence was okay. I'm sure, to many people, this sounds weird and that I'm knee deep in the crystals and woo-woo, but when you are searching for solutions to feel better and find one that works, you learn to let go of trying to understand it. If it works, even in a placebo way, that is fine. Better is better, no matter how you get there.

"Think about it like a computer that has been programmed. We have code that makes up the patterns and programs in our bodies that is in our DNA. We have to take those things out of your body. I am un-programming the fear."

It seemed kind of simple when he explained it like that.

"I am feeling anger coming from you. There is a lot of anger in your DNA. From Toby, it's in Liam. It goes back generations."

That was probably true. Even though I didn't necessarily feel angry, I knew there was *something* there.

"Anger constricts everything. It tightens, and it is the reason for the pain you are feeling in your neck. As we work through it together, you will feel it lift. There is also fear, and this fear will change over time as I work through your body. Growth is about maturing and understanding. Putting things together so you can say, 'I get it.' Every layer of 'getting it' builds a newer understanding."

When you hear the truth, it resonates, like a tuning fork. And this was resonating deep in my soul. I nodded quietly.

He continued in his quiet, sage way. "You agreed with being in the background in work and relationships because you have never owned yourself. You didn't believe in yourself enough. Recent events have been crippling in every way. You will need to clear everything so you can reconstruct yourself to get to the natural state of who you are."

Tears came. This happened so much with Noah. When he found the vein of truth and exposed it, the tears unleashed and confirmed he was right. I sniffled and wiped them away with the toilet paper that was sitting on the edge of my desk.

"Insecurity and looking for inner validation leaks out onto others. You seek it because something is lacking internally. It is exhausting to you. You tell others, 'Take away my lack. Fill me up. Tell me that you approve of me, that you wouldn't leave me.' This constant ruminating is exhausting your resources. It kills your endocrine system and hormones. No one needs to give you validation or take away your fear. That has to come from inside of you."

Sweet Jesus, this man is so wise.

"This is a huge time of transition. I am digging incredibly tough stuff out of you, and this comes with the release of pain, but it leads you to a quieter place. You might need to be without a whole lot right now. The emptiness is a beautiful place for you to be because you are not with the things that caused you pain."

I never thought about it like that.

"The way we engage with other people causes us to lose so much energy. We keep pushing to make the pattern work, even if it is killing us. In relationships, there are two halves, and each needs the other to complete the pattern. These patterns are incredibly difficult to break."

He took a breath and continued calmly. "Mom stuff is coming up intensely. When you are in Scotland, reflect in your mom's shoes. When she was not talking to you for four years, what was she feeling? Reflect without criticism. This dynamic feeds into your energy with Liam. You can relate to a lot of what he is going through. He feels the same way you did when your mom withdrew. When she isolated. Why is it easy to isolate ourselves? Why the division?"

At first, I didn't get it. My mom made the choice to isolate herself. I didn't think I did that with Liam since I withdrew to protect myself and Josie.

Wait. Fuck. He is right. This hurts.

More ugly crying commenced.

"Reflect in her shoes," he repeated gently.

"I will do that."

"I can't wait to hear how Scotland has changed you. Much strength to you, Ninya. Remember to connect to the earth. Ground your body as much as you are able. This will be an amazing experience for you."

He closed the call, and I sobbed for nearly an hour.

TWELVE

I made one final call to Erika before we left. When I look back at it now, we actually only spoke on the phone a total of three times. Crazy. I know.

"How much cash should I bring?" I asked. I had no idea what was normal. I had never left the country before, not even to go to Mexico or Canada.

"I'm bringing $1500, and I'll exchange it over there."

"*Dollars?*" I asked, shocked at the amount.

She laughed at my stunned response. "Yes, dollars. I don't have a credit card. I pay for everything with cash."

I was stunned.

No credit card at all? Who does that? What about emergencies?

"I am not comfortable carrying that much cash on me," I admitted. Visions of Scotland teeming with sophisticated pickpockets fleecing naive travelers like me filled my head.

"You don't have to. That's just how much I bring. Should last me the whole two weeks."

"Really?"

It still seemed crazy to me, but then she changed the subject to what clothing to bring, and it never came up again.

We were going to travel to Scotland for two weeks with nothing more than carry-on luggage. People that know me laughed at the prospect of this. I was a chronic over-packer. During our five-day girl's trip to New Orleans, I checked luggage and endured the ridicule, mostly because I needed to bring my fan for the white noise that was necessary to sleep. This was going to be a challenge. A backpack and a carry-on, that was all I was going to take for two weeks. It was going to be cold, so I had to pack a rain coat, for sure, and many layers to take on and off while we hiked. Packing was the ultimate puzzle, and Marie Kondo's *"Life Changing Magic of Tidying Up"* book was hitting a fever pitch. I could only stomach one episode of her Netflix show; talking to clothing always felt a little strange to me, but she was fascinating. How does someone navigate this world we live in and still preserve her sweetness like that? She really is an anomaly and just made me feel unworthy while I watched her roll up her tiny t-shirts.

On Black Friday, I scored a great backpack that still brings me joy in the weirdest ways to this day. Little pockets and hidden zippers all over the thing, in my favorite color, teal. It had a way to neatly store everything I needed to take with me. We were trying to pack as light as possible, so only items that were needed made the cut. Mere wants had to be sacrificed. Always conscious of the weight because I knew I would be personally carrying it often, I was ruthless with cutting items, and it actually was quite freeing in a way. When the backpack first arrived on my doorstep, I took one look at it and thought, *there is no way I can fit everything I need for two weeks in this and a carry on.* It seemed impossible without a shrink ray gun.

I bought a keyboard for my iPad and made a makeshift writing station, and Ryan helped me get the offline version of Google docs installed so I could write anywhere I wanted, with or without an internet connection. And bonus, it fit into the flat zipper section near my back in the most satisfying way. The organization nerd in me who loves the container store was overjoyed. Every pound mattered. I was going to have to wear that backpack most days, and everything was slimmed down to fit.

The week before, Ryan handed me a phone.

"I had Google Fi installed on this, and I want you to take it for emergencies."

"Aww, babe." My heart exploded, I wasn't used to men doing things to take care of me or make my life easier, and each thing he did always melted me.

"Stop it," he teased me.

"I can't, babe. The hearty eyes are coming for you hard." I batted my eyelashes at him and tried to look up at him alluringly.

He laughed. It was our inside joke. I am a walking, heart-eyed emoticon. He always marveled at why the little things he did meant so much to me.

I hugged him. "I can't wait until we get to take a trip like this."

"Me too." His arms always felt strong, safe, and capable.

The night before the trip, it was really getting tight. I rolled my clothing up, and was ready to wear my hiking shoes onto the plane, along with a few layered sweatshirts Joey Tribbiani style. If it didn't fit in the carry-on, I either had to wear it, or it had to go. I had to be ruthless in what I brought. It was the only way. I wore four layers on the plane, but I didn't care. I was going to Scotland. I was going to finally use my passport, and I was going to get that passport stamp. I was going to have a life-changing experience on a mountaintop. I was ready for it.

THIRTEEN

Ryan drove me to the airport. I was a bundle of nerves, having had that nightmare where you are at the airport but don't have your passport. Jittery already, a wrong turn ratcheted up the anxiety. I was worried I wouldn't have enough time. I was worried I had to check in at the desk, even though I was traveling with a carry-on and had already done the pre-check-in procedure online. I worried, I worried, I worried. It's what I was used to, and my brain had a hard time functioning without the added activity of worry.

I hugged him at the curb and kissed him goodbye, wearing sunglasses to hide my tears. He hugged me tight, reaching in between my backpack and my body to squeeze me.

"Have a great time, sweetheart. I love you." It was strange hearing him say that. He didn't say it often. Not one for ending every phone call with it, those words were reserved for real moments and always surprised me and meant so much.

He handed me my carry-on, and I walked away from him,

wiping the tears from behind my glasses. I took one more glance back at him and then rolled my way into the airport. After making it through security, I got a salad and a Jalapeño Pineapple Mule at a restaurant to calm my nerves. It felt decadent to only have to worry about myself. For the next two weeks, I wasn't a mother, or a business partner, or a girlfriend. I was just me, embarking on the adventure of a lifetime.

I sipped the mule slowly and watched a table of four women in their sixties, laughing and teasing each other, waiting for their own adventure to begin.

I want that someday.

Feeling strange sitting in an airport alone, the quiet gave me time to think about why I was doing something like this in the first place. I had been in survival mode, ruled by fear, for so long.

Afraid of what people will think.
Afraid of not being enough.
Afraid they would see the truth and not like what they saw.
Afraid of being alone.
Afraid of going all in on my own projects and finding my own success.
Afraid of failure.

Fear just sucked the life out of me. It forced me to play small and shrink myself, to minimize my talents and gifts. I yearned to break out of that self-imposed prison in the worst way, and Scotland was going to do that for me. I chewed on the truth slowly, and it was harder to swallow than my cobb salad. Another sip of the mule and I tried to frame it more positively. When you know what you don't want, it becomes easier to see what you do. I mentally tallied my truths and kept them at the forefront of my mind.

What do I need?
I need clearer boundaries.
I need to remove distractions.
I need to do more things I love.
I need to travel more. Traveling fills me up.
I need to embrace the body I have and love it as it is.
I need to stop looking for validation outside myself.

What do I want?
I want joy, clarity, faith in myself and my abilities.
I want peace and contentment and love.
I want to feel valued, supported, and deeply loved in a way
that heals my soul and in a way I have never felt before.
I want financial success and the security and peace it
brings.
I want to build or find a home that I love and that feels safe.
I want a comfortable relationship that is easy, solid, good,
and true. Full of trust, respect, love, fun, and adventure.
I want to live a creative life that fulfills me.

After lunch, it was second nature to pull up social media and to waste time there while waiting for my flight to board, but I steeled myself against it. I made the decision to stay off social media completely for the entire two weeks, and I was going to honor that decision. Social media consumed my life. I used my career as an excuse, but if I was honest, going on to post something for the business "really quick" became liking a funny meme and then down into the internet rabbit hole for hours. Instead, I posted before I left that I was "closed for spiritual maintenance," and I was going to be true to that decision. Just take a full break. Spending hours and hours online had become automatic, but the authentic connections I deeply desired I would never be able to find in the shallow fakery that is social media. Instead, I planned to read and write and get my head clear about what was next for me. Figure out how to unwind from the stress of the last three years. Process all the unresolved feelings that were holding me back and shut the door.

I scored the middle seat on the eight-hour flight. I didn't even care. I was going to *Scotland*. It was happening. After waiting nearly a year and a half from the time I said yes to the day I boarded the aircraft, it always seemed so far away, like it was just a thought. Scotland was just *someplace* I was going to go *someday*, but that someday was today! I felt so many things—anxiety and excitement, wonder and freedom all mixed into one. I only had to worry about myself for the next two weeks. I was just me, embarking on my own quest for enlightenment.

I was seated between two ladies. Looking around, I saw that the flight was nearly one-hundred-percent female.

To my left was a woman who was reading on a kindle with type so large there were only about fifty words on each page. To my right was a sweet lady who scored the window seat.

"Would you like one?" She pulled an antibacterial wipe from her purse and proceeded to wipe the tray and her armrests. "Can't be too careful." She wiped everything with a second, fresh wipe. "You never know when they cleaned these things last."

I accepted a wipe because social code dictates you have to. It would have been like refusing a breath mint. When someone offers one, you must always take it.

I noticed a little emblem on the shirts of many of the women on this flight. It looked like mountains and said Peaker. All the women were laughing and chatting and carrying on like they had known each other forever.

"Is this your first trip to Scotland?" I tried to make small talk with the lady next to me.

"Heavens, no! It's my sixth."

"Wow," I said. "It's such a big world, but you keep coming back here?"

"Yes, it's just incredibly beautiful. I never get tired of it. There is no other place as magical on earth." She smiled wistfully. "I'm actually coming for a gala."

"A gala?" I parroted back to her. I thought galas were reserved for Barbie movies. In my social circle, no one I knew ever attended a gala.

"Yes! It's called My Peak Challenge." She leaned in closer, excited to share. "Have you read the *Outlander* series?"

"Funny you ask that because I just downloaded the first book." It seemed like required reading when you went to Scotland. I loved to read and had nothing but time due to my social media fast, so it was sitting unopened on my iPad.

"Well, the character of Jamie is played by Sam Heughan, and he is the founder of My Peak Challenge. It's not just a club; it's a *movement,* and every year they have a gala in Edinburgh. People come from all over the world for this event."

The germaphobe next to me chimed in. "This is my first year, but he has truly changed my life. I've lost twenty-two pounds." I was impressed, having weighed nearly two hundred myself at one point. Losing sixty of it was one of the biggest accomplishments of my life.

"Losing weight is so hard," I commiserated with her. "How did you do it?"

"The boring way, eating right and exercising." She laughed, and I laughed with her because I knew too well it was the only way that worked long-term.

She continued on. "My Peak Challenge is a training and nutrition program where we support and challenge each other, but it's not just that because Sam has raised nearly two million dollars for charities all over the world. He's just incredible." She was practically swooning and literally fanning herself. I wasn't sure if it was because he was hot, or because she was.

That nutrition program must include the Sam Heughan is a God Kool-aid.

"This conference includes a meet and greet and a gala and a special workout that Sam leads. He's just an amazing human being," she gushed. She clearly was in love with Sam Heughan.

"I have been chosen to introduce him," the sweet older lady to my left said. "So, I've got the next eight hours to figure out the words to say to introduce the man who has completely changed my life."

"Yes!" She went on. "It's an incredible organization. He's really affecting change on a global level."

Great. I am stuck between two evangelists at a Sam Heughan-is-the-greatest-human-in-the-world presentation.

"We have a Facebook group, and everyone is just so awesome and supportive. It really is a *family*."

"And how much does it cost to be in this *family*?" I asked skeptically.

"It wasn't much," she defended, quickly changing the topic. "Nearly every penny is donated to charity. *He is changing lives,*" she stressed so incredibly seriously I had to cover my mouth to stifle a giggle.

Is this a cult? It sounds like a cult. I am trapped on an airplane for the next eight hours with the Sam Heughan cult.

Luckily for me, headphones exist. It was an overnight flight, which meant I could close my eyes and pretend to sleep, and there were movies to be seen.

I put my headphones in and started scrolling through the movie options. I checked my phone for the time. *I can squeeze in three, maybe four movies during this flight.* It felt indulgent. I hadn't had that kind of uninterrupted time to myself for years, without anyone weighing in on what I chose to watch. I flipped and flipped, and then one movie stopped me cold.

Beautiful Boy.

FOURTEEN

Several months ago, I sent a text with a link to my son.

Me: Beautiful Boy, the new movie with Steve Carrell.
Want to go see this?

A few seconds later, a text came back.

Liam: Don't send anything like this to me ever again.

I was used to the short jugular responses from him. He was angry, so angry with me. He was so angry with his dad, with life. The beautiful boy I gave birth to hated my guts. He blamed me. He wanted nothing to do with me, and that pain is like nothing I can ever accurately describe, so exquisitely consuming, layered in guilt, shame, and fear. Like having your heart laid bare and then stabbed with a sharp needle, over and over again. Fresh sharp stabs, at nearly every interaction, and yet I always thought the next one might be different, might be better.

I blamed myself. I blamed myself for marrying an alcoholic. For not valuing myself enough to demand a healthy partner. I blamed myself for choosing an addict to father my children, knowing that their DNA was like a time bomb with the genetic tendency to follow in their father's footsteps. I watched them like a hawk, hyper-vigilant, looking for signs of addiction. The ultimate helicopter parent, I hovered and overcompensated. I watched episode after episode of *Intervention* on TLC, sorting and cataloging the signs and signals of addiction. I even forced them to watch it with me, thinking that the after-school specials I was forced to endure in the 80s were so pivotal in my own decisions not to do drugs.

I got married, had two kids, and then I numbed out to the reality of my life. I had made a commitment to a man and had children who depended on me. Divorce wasn't in my wheelhouse since I was raised Catholic and was traditionally minded. I pushed my wants and feelings aside and settled into a life sentence with an addict. I had made my bed, so I was resolved to lie in it because I did not want my kids to come from a broken home. That philosophy worked for nearly two decades, and then I turned forty and woke up. It was like I'd been in a coma, and then I was awake, and my eyes were opened to the misery I was in.

There is something that happens with your internal clock when you hit middle age. Panic sets in because you know you are halfway done. Time no longer spools out to infinity for you; there is a finite amount available, and you've already used up half. The good half, the young half, the easy half. At forty, I was finally desperate enough to do something about it.

I chose myself. The selfish choice. As a mother, you're not

supposed to do that, but I did it anyway. I asked for a divorce when my children were ten and fourteen. I tried to stay, but looking at the unhappiness filling nearly every corner of my life, knowing they would move on to live their own lives while I remained stuck and unhappy, I chose myself.

Kids are resilient. That's what everyone will tell you when you are going through a divorce. It's not true. Oprah's show on kids and divorce that I watched in the 90s was actually the most accurate. It changes who they are. Forever. It really does.

I just couldn't do it anymore. So, I chose myself, and in doing so, I broke them. I broke my children. And I will forever wish I could go back in time and fix it, but I can't. There is only now and the reality of today, and beating yourself up doesn't get you anywhere.

FIFTEEN

I hated myself and punished myself for many things. But one event, sixteen months before Scotland, nearly destroyed me. One event changed everything I thought I knew about myself, what I was capable of, and what kind of person I had become.

Hyperemesis gravidarum, that's what it is called. I didn't know the real name; I just knew that I wanted to die. There is the typical morning sickness that most women have suffered through, and then there is hyperemesis gravidarum. Like morning sickness on steroids, it lands you in the hospital for dehydration nearly weekly, and it lasts all day and for nearly the *entire* pregnancy, making everyday tasks impossible. I had the same condition when I was pregnant with my son, and so I knew what it felt like. But the circumstances this time were vastly different. I was married before and without children and responsibilities, so if I needed to lay in bed for days, I could. If I needed a ride to the hospital, I had one. This time, I had neither, and I was miserable and alone.

Lying in bed in my apartment, puking for days, dehydrated and crawling to the toilet, I was so sick. The pounding migraine from the dehydration coupled with the soreness from the constant vomiting was a debilitating condition. I couldn't work, I couldn't eat, I couldn't parent, and I barely slept. If you have never experienced this, you don't know how miserable a human being can truly be.

I reached out to a friend to bring me fruit. I craved it so intensely, pineapple especially, mostly because of the dehydration, and I survived on that and English muffins that I dragged myself to the kitchen to toast between vomiting sessions.

My kids could see I was very sick, so they helped with the dog, and I begged my son to be good at school because I was so sick and needed him to toe the line. I told him that I couldn't handle any more problems right now. Two days later, he was suspended for vaping. The conversation we had after that incident left me reeling.

He sat on the sofa, defiant and angry. My ex-husband and I were trying to have a talk with him about the consequences of his actions. He was strung tight, flexed and anxious. I sat quietly, leaning back into an almost laying down position, and prayed that I wouldn't have to excuse myself to throw up.

"Why?" I asked. "You know I'm not feeling well. This is unacceptable."

His leg bounced up and down, trying to dispel the extra energy. He was keyed up, impulsive, and not willing to admit he had screwed up. So, he made me the scapegoat.

"A crack whore would be a better mother than you," he spit at me. As I focused on a spot on the coffee table, my mouth watering, I breathed slowly, trying to quell the rolling of the acid in my belly.

"You make me sick, always looking for sympathy. Every

man you chose leaves you because they can't stand you. You've ruined my life and Josie's life."

He was shaking and screaming. He was lashing out at me for destroying his life, and honestly, he had a few valid points. But the disrespect and anger coming at me then hurt so intensely, it was hard to see the little boy who was just *sad*. So sad that his life was so painful and in constant upheaval when being a regular fifteen-year-old in the best circumstances was hard enough.

He slammed the door and left with his dad, and I crawled back to bed.

I barely moved from my bed for two weeks. Out of desperation, I reached out to Cal. I went to his house with the positive pregnancy test and handed it to him. At first, he didn't believe me.

"How can this be true? I had a vasectomy." He was stunned.

"It's yours, Cal. You're the only man I've been with."

"How can this be? Maybe it's a false positive."

"This is my third test," I verified stoically.

He was quiet, in shock. We both were. "What are the odds?"

"A billion to one," I proposed sadly, looking out the window again, wanting to be a bird again so I could fly away from this mess.

"I honestly thought I was late because it was early menopause, but decided to take a test to be sure. I am just as floored as you are."

"What do you want to do?"

"I don't know. I guess I better start with vitamins." My catholic guilt forced me to surrender to this cosmic twist of fate. I let Cal back into my life because of this baby. I needed support, and to his credit, after finally accepting the truth, he tried to help me. I texted Cal to bring me things like food and toilet paper. I couldn't keep the prenatal vitamins down; I couldn't keep anything down. He was uncomfortable, not sure what to do or how to handle the situation, seeing me so sick. Beyond the regular food drops, he stayed away out of fear, focusing on work like he always did. I was alone so much with my own fears that played over and over on auto-loop in my head.

I'm forty-three. The risk for birth defects from my ancient eggs and his aged sperm is incredibly high. How in the hell did this even happen? He's had a vasectomy for over a decade. What are the chances that it would just spontaneously heal itself ten years later?

Minuscule is the answer, but it did.

We were responsible. We initially talked about birth control, but with his vasectomy didn't think we'd ever need it. How did this even fucking happen?

The idea of eighteen more years of mothering when the first go had nearly killed me was like a death sentence. It hung heavy, and I was scared and sick, so sick it was difficult to see the future and not want to die.

I was raised Catholic. Abortion was never an option. It was a black and white truth, with no room for gray. I never believed it was an option for me, either, until I was put into this situation. Out of desperation, with my mouth sour with the taste of toothpaste-flavored vomit, I googled Planned Parenthood and the abortion pill. I carefully considered all the options. Adoption was quickly eliminated as a solution because my kids would never understand my choice to give away their half-sibling. It would hurt them even more and break them again. It would make them lose faith in me further and wonder if I was capable of abandoning them.

A fight broke out between my values and my morality. When your values are only theories, it is easy to see the right path. It's easy to say, "I would never." When they are cruel realities with consequences that will span decades, the choices are much more difficult. I read and I researched. Eight weeks is when the embryo starts to develop pain receptors.

Right now, I am six weeks, two days. If I take it before eight weeks, the baby will feel no pain.

It was easier to swallow but didn't *ever* make it right. *Not ever.*

On the cold, tile floor of the bathroom, I begged God to make me miscarry, to take the decision out of my hands, and then I felt guilty about friends I knew that were devastated by miscarriage and infertility. To have this impossible decision taken out of my hands by miscarriage would have been a tender mercy. But I've never been given tender mercies, and life wasn't about to start handing them out now.

If I am going to do this, I need to do it now. I can't live with the idea of suction ripping my baby out of my uterus or knowing that it was a fetus now and could feel pain.

I stewed and stewed on it, getting weaker by the day, my resolve to stand by my values wearing down with each vomiting session and each migraine until I made the decision to terminate the pregnancy. The decision brought some peace, but also so much emotional pain. It was just another painful burden and journey in this stage of life that had already hit me so hard, taken so much, and given so little.

I had no resources. My success rate as a mother was nearly zero. I was completely depleted. Empty. A shell of what I once was. Desperate. Alone.

I am at rock bottom. Emotionally bankrupt. I am a Lifetime original movie.

SIXTEEN

"We are going to hell," Cal stated as he drove me to Planned Parenthood. He supported my choice, but he was hurting, too. We both were trying to come to grips with what was about to happen.

"You didn't make this decision. I did," I countered, trying to take the weight of this decision off his shoulders. It was true. I did.

"I'm just so sad." He looked at me, his eyes wet and glossy like a sad puppy. "We could do it," he claimed somberly. "It would be an uphill battle, but it wouldn't be the worst thing in the world."

For me, it would be. I would never survive this. The children I have now would suffer even more. It is not fair to them, and it is not fair to this baby. I have nothing to give this baby, and I would destroy its life like I did Liam and Josie's.

But I said nothing more, and so he continued to drive us quietly. We were both lost in our own thoughts of the moral ramifications of what we were going to do. I was going to end a life, and tears never stopped rolling down my face.

I nibbled on bits of bagel, trying to keep it down, not

wanting to throw up in the car. The dry heaves had worn out my stomach muscles. A block from Planned Parenthood, a purposefully placed billboard caught my eye. "Abortion is murder." I agreed, and the guilt hit hard in another wave. There were protesters outside Planned Parenthood, and I avoided eye contact, looking down in shame as we entered the building quickly.

I went to the counter. The man behind the bulletproof glass looked at me, asking for ID.

"I have an appointment."

He buzzed me into the building where I had to check in.

"I have an appointment at eleven for the abortion pill." I said it so quietly, I had to repeat it for the male clerk, surprised to see a man working the counter. My voice cracked and broke. Tears ran down my face.

Cal walked to a chair in the waiting room, sat down, and sighed, then we waited until my name was called.

"Can he come with me?" I asked, wanting some support.

"No, it's protocol. We do not allow anyone in the ultrasound room." The nurse answered.

I looked back at Cal as he sat in the chair, head down, defeated, and then she whisked me into a room. I wondered how many women she had done this with recently. It was all just so sad and surreal to me.

"Do you want to hear the heartbeat or know if there are multiples?" she asked when I was in the gown with my feet in the cold metal stirrups.

"No," I replied, the tears falling fast. I knew I wouldn't be able to go through with it if I knew. I needed some modicum of detachment if I was ever going to be able to live with my decision.

She inserted the instrument inside me for the ultrasound, and I felt dirty and violated, like trash. With tears still running down my face, I was desperate for this procedure to end. Wishing she would say, "That's weird, there is nothing here. Are you sure you are pregnant?" She probed me internally while looking on the monitor, and I couldn't bring myself to look. Even the hazy screen with the faint black and white blobs was too real for me, and I couldn't bear to look at it.

"You are seven weeks one day," she confirmed matter-of-factly.

I nodded in agreement; I already knew. It had happened the night before I moved out.

"Are you making this decision for yourself, and no one is influencing you?"

"Yes," I said quietly, wiping the tears from my face and having a hard time breathing.

"Get dressed, please, and the doctor will see you in a minute."

I waited in the consultation room, looking at all the posters for birth control options. I read the booklet I was given about the abortion pill and what would happen next.

The doctor came in shortly after. "You are completely sure about your decision, and no one has influenced it?"

"Yes."

She handed me a bottle of medication. "You will take this one now in front of me. This will stop the flow of the pregnancy hormone to the embryo. Then tomorrow morning, you will take the other two that will expel the tissue."

I looked at it a long time before I swallowed. I never thought this would happen to me. I never thought I would have to make a decision like this. I never thought my life would ever lead me here.

I'm so sorry, baby. I have nothing I can give you right now, and the cost is too high. Forgive me.

I swallowed it with a glass of water and went to Cal's

house to sleep. It was a long night of tossing and turning, knowing the worst part was still to come.

The next morning, I took the other pills. Scared that I would throw them up, I waited until I'd vomited everything out of my stomach that morning. They tasted like nothing, pulpy and papery, and I laid back down on the bed, my head pounding, the tears falling fast again. I hugged the pillow and buried myself under blankets, apprehensive and not knowing what to expect. I couldn't bear the idea of having to repeat the process, so I focused on keeping them down. I watched the clock, the minutes ticking by painfully slow, nausea increasing with each passing second. Breathing slowly, eating small bites of crackers and drinking small sips of water, I struggled to keep them down, my stomach sour. Five minutes after the time I was required to keep them down in order to avoid having to repeat the process, the vomiting started.

Violent vomiting. It was thick and choking me, coming through my mouth and nose, and I gagged and gagged.

This is what I deserve. I am a horrible human being.

A few hours after that, intense cramps and bleeding began. I stayed on the toilet, hugging a garbage can to my chest for the vomiting, while I wished that there was someone there. I wished Cal had taken the day off work to take care of me. I wanted my mom. I wished she was still alive, but I knew she would have been so disappointed in me, so I wouldn't have been able to ask for her help anyway. I wanted someone to lean on who would help me through this impossible task. But I didn't ask because I didn't think I deserved it. I didn't deserve to have someone hold my hand when I had brought all this on myself. I didn't deserve any kind of comfort or relief. There was no one. I was utterly alone. The vomiting this time was different, like poison coming out of me. It was horrific. I bled and bled, so much blood, so many fluids depleted from my system, and after several hours, I was so thirsty and hungry and weak. Hours later, my legs numb from sitting on the cold porcelain, I crawled to the bed on my hands and knees, and it took several minutes to recover from the effort of that task alone.

Later that night, Cal came home from work. We were watching TV when I asked for water. It was the first and only thing I asked of him. I was so thirsty after that ordeal; every fluid had been depleted, and I needed it *now*. It was an urgent, all-consuming need, and I couldn't wait. He sat there without moving, not even acknowledging my request, watching his show. I waited and waited, desperate for it. The need for it became so strong I couldn't physically ignore it any longer. I pulled myself out of bed and started crawling to the bathroom.

"What are you doing?"

"I need water now. I can't wait anymore," I answered, frustrated, and continued to crawl weakly to the bathroom.

"I was going to get it after this episode."

After this episode? What in the fuck? I was livid. That one statement summed up our entire relationship and completely justified my decision to leave him.

The next morning, I woke up at four thirty a.m. and snuck out of his house for the final time. I got in my Jeep and drove myself back to my apartment. A few days later, the constant nausea that had nearly killed me for the last several weeks was gone, and I was equal parts relieved and ashamed, and ashamed for feeling relieved.

SEVENTEEN

During an eight-hour flight on United, they feed you nearly constantly. I guess they want to avoid people getting hangry in a confined area. Probably a smart plan considering we were barreling through the atmosphere in the tiny, cramped space that is economy class. Being in the middle seat, I tried to strategically plan my trips to the bathroom in order to inconvenience the least amount of people. I calculated how much water I should have in order to avoid having to wake up my seat mates during the night, but also needing to avoid the migraine that I knew would come if I got dehydrated. I slept and walked around in socks—gross, I know, but sleeping in the stiff hiking shoes that weren't quite broken in enough seemed impossible. I was surprised and grateful that the time passed so quickly. I spent the rest of the time reading a bit, and then the seatbelt light dinged.

"Ladies and gentlemen."

There were no gentlemen on the flight; it was just a formality.

"We are now beginning our descent into Edinburgh. Please return to your seats and fasten your seatbelts.

The sun was coming up, and I looked out the window. Water connected by tiny bridges and vast fields of yellow and green. So much yellow and green. I later found out that the yellow was from the Scottish mustard crop, but I had never seen fields of it before from the air and it was beautiful.

I was in Scotland.

The women next to me busied themselves with getting their belongings together, and we chit-chatted about where to go and what to see. Once I got past the Sam Heughan infatuation, they were really very nice people. I added a few notes to my phone about things they suggested and then felt the wheels touch down. Clutching the customs form and my passport in my hand, I walked off the aircraft to go through customs and get my stamp. The coveted passport stamp, it was my first ever, and I was nearly giddy with anticipation. The line was tiny, and in record time, I was in front of a burly, bulldog-like officer, telling him I was just visiting and planned on staying in an Airbnb with my friend Erika. He barely looked up, bored with the response, reached for the metal stamp, and touched it to the ink pad. Then I heard the distinctive metallic mechanical thump, and there it was, my stamp. I had fought long and hard for it. I could finally call myself a world traveler.

Walking quickly to the bathroom to freshen up, since airplane bathrooms always make me feel a little claustrophobic, I wanted to wash my face and brush my teeth. Then I was going to use WhatsApp to find Erika.

I texted Erika.

I'm here, where are you?

I was nervous because I had never used WhatsApp and wasn't sure if it was working properly. Minutes ticked by and nothing.

I should have tested it. I'll be stuck in this airport forever.

I waited in front of Starbucks but needed to walk after being confined in a seat for the last several hours and wanted to stretch my legs. So, I dragged my suitcase behind me, looking for her, and then I saw a door leading outside and walked through it to get some air. The silver Edinburgh sign was huge near the trains. I pulled out my phone and snapped a few quick photos, waiting for a response. Sending more texts through WhatsApp, I was getting worried we weren't going to connect. Finally, I received a message from Erika, and after nearly twenty minutes of back and forth messages, the automatic doors opened and, in a whoosh of air, there she was, a huge smile on her face, her dark brown eyes sparkling.

This was the first time I met Erika.

We hugged and laughed, both shocked a little that this was finally happening and that we had found each other 3700 miles from home.

She was over six-foot-tall and athletic. Wearing workout wear and a baseball cap that her curly jet-black hair was spilling out the back of, she walked with purpose and confidence. She didn't just walk, she strode, so I picked up my pace to stay even with hers. She looked amazing for nearly fifty, with an ass you could probably bounce a quarter off of, and I felt a little misshapen and jiggly next to her.

Following her, I wheeled my luggage to a kiosk that was selling train tickets.

"I need to get my money exchanged, and then I'll pay you back," she said matter-of-factly.

I didn't think anything of it, inserted my card, and added two train tickets. We boarded the next train and zipped through the scenery on our way to the city center of Edinburgh.

I drank in the sights, only half-listening to Erika's story

about her near miss at the airport in Dublin. In danger of nearly missing her flight, she had to run dramatically through the airport, like I only thought happened in movies.

"And it's only because I am in *such* amazing shape that I was able to run like that. They held the plane for me, and when I got on board, everyone clapped. They clapped for me! I asked to be moved because I wanted a window seat, and then they sat me next to this baby that screamed the entire time. It was torture."

The train weaved and chugged through backyards of adorable stone houses with clotheslines that had morning wash on them. Everything was incredibly lush and green. As we got closer to town, the scenery changed. There were old stone buildings with flower window baskets brimming with petunias and ivy and bordered with wooden shutters. Picturesque. It's the only accurate way to describe it, like going back in time to a completely different world. I was excited.

We grabbed our luggage and got out at our stop near the Royal Mile. I was like a baby duck blindly following its mother, and I was grateful she knew where to go. Enormous stone and wrought iron buildings that were over five hundred years old were set on cobblestone streets with red phone booths that dotted the curbs. Erika had booked our first Airbnb right on the Royal Mile, the most famous street in all of Edinburgh. We dragged our luggage up, up, and up the uneven sidewalks and cobblestone streets. I was getting winded fast and wanted to stop over and over to marvel at the sheer beauty of the place. But I also needed to catch my breath because, at one point, I was pretty sure I was dying. Just the one uphill walk to the Airbnb had destroyed any illusion that I was in any kind of shape to climb the mountains of Scotland, but I didn't want Erika to know. I was huffing and puffing like it was my job, struggling to keep up with her as she effortlessly climbed the steep sidewalks and terrain with calves that looked like they had been chiseled from granite. At busy intersections, double decker green and yellow city buses whizzed by. Part of me died inside, wishing we could get on one to make the trek to the flat easier. The other part was thankful the heavy traffic gave me an excuse to catch my breath without having to ask for a break. For whatever reason, I wanted to prove myself to this woman, and I didn't want to be labeled a whiner this early on in the trip.

Suck it up, buttercup.

I pushed my burning calves and breathed in the city air punctuated by diesel fuel. Everything was ornate and made of stone and just oozed beauty. We finally found our flat after walking what felt like two miles uphill and stored the luggage at the bottom of the spiral staircase while we waited for our room to be ready. Then I grabbed my camera and my wallet, and we headed out for our first day to explore, both of us exhausted from barely sleeping on the overnight flight over.

"I have to exchange my money for pounds," she said, and we walked to the money exchange center, not far from our flat.

I planned on using my credit card for everything, as much as I could, and had a little to exchange for pounds, but she needed to exchange money immediately since she'd only brought cash.

I stood next to her while she tried to negotiate a better currency conversion fee while a line six people deep formed behind us. She was trying to save pennies, and the patient lady with the sweet accent told her more than once that the rate is set daily and there was no room negotiation. Finally, she gave in and converted some of her money, holding out hope that she would find a better rate somewhere else. She was frustrated and voiced her displeasure, and the lady behind the glass tried to commiserate. God bless her, the Scots are a gracious people.

Then the teller slid the most beautiful money I had ever seen though the little silver dish, and we stuffed it in our hidden wallets. So many colors and sizes. I was used to American money, green and all a uniform size, the only difference being the numerals on the bills to differentiate. British Pounds are like art, created in beautiful colors, like magenta, teal, and blue. Some had holographic images of the queen, and the denominations were hard to understand at first. Anything less than five pounds was a coin. And don't even get me started on pence and how much that was and when you should use it. I had no idea. I just stuffed it all in my wallet that was strapped to my stomach then touched my credit card and my passport in what had become a comforting OCD ritual of sorts before zipping it shut.

Then we were back on the sidewalk, looking around.

"I need coffee," she declared, and at first, it didn't seem that would be a problem, considering there were nearly seventeen cafes within walking distance. I am certain that we literally walked into twelve of them, asking for sugar-free syrups that don't exist in the UK.

She'd burst through the cafe door, saying, "Excuse me," loud and direct. "Do you have sugar-free syrups here?" Sometimes we got the deer in the headlights look from the baristas, but sometimes they knew right away what we were talking about. Apparently, in the UK, they are considered poison. You can't even find them at Starbucks because artificial sweeteners are a mythical creature. Only in America is it okay to slowly poison your citizens with chemicals and additives.

"If I have real sugar, it messes with my system," she explained. "It literally makes me shit like a goose."

Great. Our first day here consists of the never-ending sugar-free syrup quest and listening to her bowel issues. Not exactly the incredible adventure I had romanticized in my mind for the last year and a half.

She laughed and kept walking. "I'm blunt. That's just me."

I was trying to be diplomatic and told her she might just have to go without, or even {GASP} concede to have some sugar. Eventually, she gave in and ordered a small coffee with sugar. Apparently, even she had limits when it came to wasting time.

"I hope this doesn't make me shit all night long." She sipped it carefully and then added a scone to her order.

She bit into it after slathering it with clotted cream, then closed her eyes. "Scones are just different here. They are so good." She savored it in what seemed like an almost religious experience.

I was antsy and ready to do something significant. It felt like we were wasting so much time. I was here to do *important* work.

"I need to get some toiletries. Those assholes at the airport in Dublin confiscated all of mine. They took my good shampoo."

This made me more irritated because she had specifically told me what to pack and how to pack it to avoid this very problem, but then she didn't follow her own advice.

Calm down. You're in Scotland. You're just tired and irritable. It's the jet lag.

We walked and walked, asking locals where to find a chemist. So many of them were tourists like ourselves, so it was difficult to get good directions. As a result, we got sent on many wild goose chases. Up and down alleys, exhausted and jet lagged, eventually, we found the chemist on a corner we had already circled twice.

We went in together, and I bought a plug adapter. She

agonized over her purchase. This one or that one. Hemming and hawing.

Just fucking buy one already. You are wasting so much time.

The jet lag was making me short and testy.

Finally, she got what she needed, and we were on our way to start our adventure in Scotland.

EIGHTEEN

Waiting for our flat to be ready, we had a lot of time to kill, so we decided to go to a cemetery.

Get it? Kill... Cemetery? Peace out, Edinburgh, I'm here all week.

We walked to Greyfriar's Kirkyard. The redbud trees were in full bloom, the petals kissing the cobblestones when the wind ripped them from the trees. The stones and patina were breathtaking, all the ironwork and mausoleums. It was hauntingly beautiful. You can feel that it is a sacred place. Everywhere I looked was a photo, and I tried to take them all. Literally.

"You're going to run out of storage if you continue to take photos like this every day," Erika remarked, laughing at me.

It *was* pretty ridiculous. She would lead the way, and then I would fall behind, enamored by this epitaph or that old wooden door. There was so much beauty, my eyes had a hard time taking it all in. Every ten feet, I was stopping and taking a photo. At this rate, we'd never even leave Edinburgh. It would take up the entire two weeks on its own.

The views were stunning. I saw a castle high on the hill—
a real-life castle. Since I was a little girl, I was fascinated with
castles, kings, and queens, and that romantic time period
made me swoon.

"We aren't going to go through that one, but we'll spend a
day at Stirling Castle. It's one of the most beautiful castles in
Scotland."

We walked the streets and met up with an acquaintance
of hers that was a Peaker and in town for the Gala, a very
sweet, older, single lady.

Hungry, we were trying to find something open for lunch
at ten a.m. After being up all night, our body clocks were off.
We stumbled onto a patio that overlooked the most beautiful
row of pastel colored antique town houses in Edinburgh.
Probably one of the most Instagrammed spots in the city.

Maxie's Bistro's stone garden terrace was nestled high on
this famous street. I took a chair facing the view, so ready to
sit down after all the walking we had done in the cemetery. I
was still getting used to seeing the amazing stonework on
nearly every structure. The city was a jewel box of architecture, each building more ornate and showy than the last. The
owner took our easy orders quickly.

"Fish and Chips all around."

My stomach growled as I listened to the friends talk
about Scotland and what they were seeing and where they
were planning to hike. None of it made any sense to me. I
was just happy to be sitting down and joyful that food was on
the way.

"You're a Peaker?" I asked.

"Yes," her friend said. "But I'm not as fanatical as the
others."

"My flight was filled with them. Nice people, but I have to
say, it seems a little like a cult," I mused.

She smiled. "There's been some drama around how much

access to Sam we will get. Last year, he only ran out onto the field for the parade and then disappeared for the rest of the weekend. He's so very busy, you know, doing so much good with his charity." She was busy making excuses for him.

I was starting to see that he recruited a type. Single, middle-aged women, possibly with a few cats, who read the books and fell in love with his character, Jamie, in the *Outlander* series.

"Have you seen him?" Erika asked me.

"No. I haven't seen the show."

"He's gorgeous. Long red hair, amazing body, he's so hot." She was swooning, and it was fun to see her in that state. "I like dirty Jamie the best. From season one."

"I liked them all," her friend replied, smiled, and then quietly changed the subject to the hike she wanted to take.

The fish and chips arrived. Crispy battered filets the size of my forearm. Thick chips, crispy on the outside and pillowy potato goodness on the inside. I was nearly salivating.

"I need tartar. A lot of tartar," Erika said abruptly to the owner.

He came back to the table with three small cups of tartar sauce. Erika was annoyed at their size and immediately asked for more.

I ate in silence, listening to the women chat about people I didn't know and places I hadn't been, and I was completely content. The fish was so tender and succulent, and the greasy treat was so delicious and decadent that I was in heaven. Happily, I dipped fries in tartar sauce, because ketchup is not generally available in Scotland. Salt and sauce are your condiment options. Sauce is a brown sauce, kind of barbecue reminiscent, and ketchup will almost always cost you extra if you can find it at all.

"I'm so stuffed," Erika declared after her plate was

completely empty. Then she reached over and swiped some chips off my plate. Without asking. I was shocked. Stealing food from me is an offense that potentially could lead to a fork in the hand. I'm one of five children. We are very territorial and typically eat our food hunched over, elbows out, strategically positioning glasses and bottles as a fortress to discourage interlopers. But I was completely full so I brushed it off and smirked at her gall.

"I eat clean, Ninya. I never eat like this. But it tastes so good."

I had to agree. It was incredible, and I have never had it's equal in the States.

We stuffed ourselves to bursting on the most cliché meal of them all, and it was delicious. Then we walked it off some more, finally landing in a pub across the street from our Airbnb.

She ordered a cider. I sat at the pub table, propping my head up on my hand. It was hard to stay awake that final hour. She chattered on about her husband, her horses, her kids, and all kinds of random things. I focused on keeping my eyes open and my head upright, a task that was becoming nearly impossible. Normally, Airbnbs allow you to check in early, but not this one. They said it would be ready at three p.m., and it was ready at three p.m. Overjoyed that a bed awaited us, we stumbled across the street and let ourselves in, not knowing there was a nearly six story spiral staircase ahead of us to conquer carrying luggage.

Everything in Edinburgh is stairs—spiral stairs, stone stairs—constantly punishing your calf muscles. Dragging our luggage, the spirals making us dizzy, we climbed and climbed. At the top, we had plenty of time to catch our breath. The metal skeleton keys and the multiple codes to unlock them were incredibly frustrating to figure out in our delusional state, and I nearly burst into tears. Finally, at long last, the doors opened to a bright flat. We found our room and collapsed on the beds, practically fully clothed, and slept for nearly ten hours straight. For an insomniac like me, it was magnificent.

NINETEEN

The sun poured into the tall, drafty windows that had no coverings, and I shivered a bit from the cold, not wanting to leave the warm sanctuary of the bed. Waking up in Scotland, it took a second to get my bearings. Nothing to rush to do, nothing to take care of, and the lack of urgency to take care of anything was delicious. I stretched like a cat and smiled, not being able to remember the last time the only person to consider was myself. My calf muscles ached from the nearly 17,000 steps we had taken the day before, most of them being stairs or uphill, but it was a great ache.

Coffee. I need coffee.

My body was slowly waking up, stiff from activity yet rested from sleep. I finally stumbled out into the shared kitchen and found the staple in all Scottish Airbnbs: the heated water kettle. Instant coffee is huge in Scotland, and Nescafe was something that I grew to endure and almost love during my stay there. It took a second to figure out, but eventually, I turned it on, the water boiled, and I made two cups. Stirring in copious amounts of sugar and powdered cream in mine, I took the other back to our room black for

Erika, who thankfully was packing her own artificial sweetener. No more quests for sugar-free syrups today!

Where was that when we needed it yesterday?

I like to think I'm a halfway intelligent woman, but it took nearly fifteen minutes to figure out how to turn on the hot water in the shower while I stood in the enormous tub, naked and cold. I was almost ready to give up and take a bath when the gods smiled on me, and I turned a random knob in a weird direction and was rewarded with the hot stuff. You would have thought I had found the answer to world peace; such was my joy at this tiny accomplishment. Standing in the huge glass shower, letting the water work on my sore muscles was a wonderful start to the day.

Our flat was on the sixth floor and overlooked clay tile roofs spotted with gray pigeons. I pulled out my iPhone and took yet another photo of the peeling window frame and the soft curtain with the church steeple in the distance. The topography of Scotland is so rife with hills and mountains, it really is hard to take a bad picture there. Like when a beauty queen takes a selfie, it's just always predictably gorgeous.

I was in fantastic spirits. I slept well, and I was caffeinated. I was ready to explore when I heard loud thunder. I'd packed for rain, so it didn't matter. But the thunder was getting louder, and I was curious what a Scottish squall would look like, so I walked to the huge windows overlooking the Royal Mile. Then I saw them, flashes of color, screaming down the empty streets. People milled around on the sidewalks, holding phones out, taking videos and pictures. Bright colors zoomed by. They were high-end, sexy sports cars in every shape and design, shifting fast and furious through the streets below. I'm not a car guy, but I'm pretty sure there were some Lamborghinis in the mix, so I pulled out my phone and recorded it. Loud and racing down the ancient streets, the contrast between these amazing engineered machines and the ancient cobblestones and stone buildings was remarkable. When they say a sports car can go from zero to sixty in three seconds, they aren't kidding. In five minutes, the show was over, and the crowds poured onto the streets again.

I sent the video to my son back home, knowing these cars were the things his dreams were made of. No response. But it was okay. That was not why I sent them in the first place.

TWENTY

We walked to Princes Street Garden, a garden that is tucked into the middle of the city of Edinburgh. Beautifully manicured and landscaped, it is the crown jewel of the city. In the center is a stunning fountain. Trimmed in aqua and gold leaf, pigeons flitted from one level to the next, drinking sips of flowing water and then feasting on the occasional chip that a tourist left behind. So many birds getting fat and happy on water and chips.

We took the requisite pictures in front of the fountain and rested a bit on the benches that surrounded it, watching other families snapping photos and chasing their toddlers around the fountain to prevent them from actually climbing in it.

I wish my kids were still that small. Everything seemed simpler then. I wish I could go back to that moment in time when things were easy and they were happy. I can't remember the last time I saw them truly happy.

Erika's voice yanked me out of my yearning for the past. "I need to get a new SIM card, and there is a shop over there that sells them. I can swap it out with mine and have coverage here. That way, if the GPS is wonky or we need to call home, we can."

We walked farther and then up the stairs. I sat in the sun outside the storefront, people watching as buses crammed full of tourists raced down the streets at fifteen-minute intervals. Erika walked from store to store, first finding and then negotiating the best deal. She was tough as nails and very direct. I would have just bought the first card I saw at the first store that had what I needed. About forty minutes later, she emerged triumphant with a new SIM card in place.

Wandering around more, we took photos. The alleys tucked between stone buildings went on forever, cobbled together piecemeal, while the city grew around them. I wondered what we'd find if we walked all the way down their wonky paths seemingly created by workers who had a tendency to hit the scotch hard. That was part of the charm of Edinburgh. You never knew what you'd find. If you turned down an alleyway, you might see hand carved doorways, window boxes with flowers spilling from them, a little ancient bookstore, or a coffee shop. The gothic architecture was impressive, heavy handed on the ornamentation, like a teenage girl who just learned how to apply makeup and then needs to put it *all* on just because she *can*.

The city vastly changes at dusk. Lights come on in multi-colored hues like orange and purple and blue that wash over the buildings. Some make them seem to glow from within. It is magical to walk around Edinburgh at night. The city comes alive again, but the dim light makes everything more alluring. I loved all the sculptures and art sprinkled around the city. In new spaces like we are used to in the States, very little of the budgets for public buildings are allocated for art. Edinburgh was created in a different time, when things were forged from the hands of true generational craftsmen. When old school stonework and metalwork was a tradition, and everything was created by hand. Not the mass produced, quickly constructed, dreadfully boring structures that are common in America.

I loved the city. I always felt safe walking down the streets. Every place you looked was a postcard. It was such a departure from what I was used to, and that is what made it so fascinating. It was like nothing else I had ever seen before.

TWENTY-ONE

The plan was to hike up Arthur's seat. Not technically a hike by Erika's hardcore standards, it was merely a walk in her world. For a chronic couch surfer like me, it was a hike that was only about an hour up to the summit. Arthur's Seat is an extinct volcano, dotted with hedges filled with yellow flowers and rock formations. Twenty minutes in, I was hurting, having to take a break to rest every hundred feet and catch my breath, and lamenting the lower back pain that was proving I was middle-aged. I felt the burn. Walking up the steep incline with a backpack is challenging because your core is so unbalanced. I had trained a few weeks before Scotland, wearing my backpack on the tread-mill with added weight in the form of soda cans, trying to prepare physically for the hiking, but it was obvious it was too little too late. I had a camera and water bottle in the backpack, and it weighed on me pretty heavily. My lower back was screaming. Erika went on ahead, navigating the hill with ease, stopping now and then for me to catch up. Halfway up the hill, we found the ruins of St. Anthony's

Chapel, and I took the opportunity to turn it into a much lengthier photo op than it needed to be because I was trying to rest and didn't want to tell Superwoman that it was too much for me already. The view was beautiful down into the fishing port of Leith.

It was cold and windy, but the view made it worth it. It also was the first hike of the trip, so I was feeling pretty accomplished when we got to the summit. A 360-degree panoramic view of Edinburgh was our reward for reaching the top, and there was a post that marked the highest point where a class of school children was gathered to eat snacks.

Erika jumped up onto the three-foot-tall post and asked me to take a photo for her fitness and coaching website and social media. Watching her pose on the post was surreal. She was literally on top of the world. No fear at all, she contemplated doing a handstand on the post that was only about sixteen inches across. My dark and vivid imagination got the best of me, and I saw it going very badly, her brains splattered all over the boulders that covered the top. Me trying to find a helicopter on short notice to medivac her to a hospital. Thankfully, she decided against it, and my anxiety started to dissipate.

We stopped at The World's End on the way back because we were starving and waited nearly an hour for "Scotland's Best Fish and Chips." Erika ordered it again, this time with mashed peas, and we were seated near a table of six Icelandic men on holiday. She was a social butterfly, striking up conversations with people wherever she went, a natural extrovert who lived for interactions with people. After exchanging pleasantries, she asked them, "What do you do?"

One man responded, "I am a pastry chef."

"My husband owns a pasty shop. We went to Cornwall, and I brought him to Scotland to learn all about the English technique earlier this year. Do you know what patsies are?" She was very proud of her husband and their successful restaurant business and talked about it nearly every day, with nearly every person we encountered. I am not exaggerating.

"A little meat pie?" the pastry chef said.

"Exactly." She smiled and settled right into a conversation with them.

One of the men was a fish farmer, raising salmon at a fish farm in Iceland. I was surprised, thinking Iceland was the land of seafood. To know they farm-raised them, too, shocked me.

"I live on a horse farm, and they are the most incredible animals. They know everything, so smart." She gushed about her farm again, her go-to when talking to anyone. She was proud of it, as she should've been; it was an incredible piece of property.

"Animals just show up at my farm. They instinctively know, if they are in need, I will take care of them. I don't know how they know; they just do." She launched into another story about a squirrel she saved from the brink of death, feeding it with a bulb syringe and then releasing it back into the wild. She pulled out her phone to show them pictures of the squirrel. "I just love animals." She put the phone down and asked, "Are there whales in Iceland?"

The fish farmer looked at me and winked, his eyes twinkling and slightly naughty.

"Yes. There are many whales in Iceland." He paused for emphasis. "Baby whales are especially tasty."

Tasty? Wait, did he just say tasty?

I started to choke on my pot pie, then I met his eyes, mine widening, his unable to contain the glee. I pressed my lips together to hide the smile that fought to break out.

Erika was stunned. "You... you eat them?" She choked the words out, looking like she might vomit.

"Yes, they are quite tender. When they are adults, they toughen up and the meat is not as good," he explained like he was talking about a common farmhouse chicken.

Erika was shocked and appalled, having a hard time swallowing the rest of her massive fish portion. Her eyes were huge.

The men fed off her reaction, looking at each other, and started sniggering a little, but she was so shocked, she was oblivious.

"Yes, baby whale tastes good. It's very delicious, but baby puffin is better," the youngest of the brothers chimed in. And then the whole table burst into laughter. Not able to contain the amusement anymore, they were rolling, nearly crying.

Then Erika finally got the joke and laughed along with them. "You're giving me shit?"

"Yes. We are giving you shit," they said in their lilting accents.

Suddenly, Iceland jumped to the top of my list of must-see destinations. Then the men spoke to each other in their native language, I would have given my right arm to understand what they were saying. I'm pretty sure they were talking about these gullible Americans who would believe anything.

We wrapped up lunch and walked back to the flat, stopping at a Tesco for a few things. Grocery stores in Scotland aren't the enormous shopping clubs we are used to in the States. They are tucked into the stone buildings and are usually very small. The hummus in Scotland was life-changing. I was so used to chemically laden hummus, filled with additives and preservatives that we have in the States. One look on the back of the package explained why it was so good. You could read and understand every ingredient without requiring a degree in food sciences. Nearly every food I ate in Scotland tasted better, and I fell in love with the soups and simple sandwiches they make there. Brie, bacon, and cranberry sandwiches, gooey and melty, are truly the thing dreams are made of.

That night, we decided to look for a pub with live music. We stumbled into a pub with a band that was singing old school cover tunes from the 80s and 90s.

Erika dressed to go out in a leather jacket and booties and tight jeans. For a woman half a century old, she looked incredible. She had muscles for days, the kind you get only by spending hours a day in the gym. I was dressed for comfort and had my "dress up" leggings on, stretchy and comfortable, still wrapped in the raincoat and hiking shoes.

We were the oldest women in the bar by far, which was fine with me. I grabbed a stool in the bar because I was exhausted from having walked nearly a million steps uphill. It was the only stool left in the place, so I am not ashamed to say that, when Erika wanted to move to the other side of the bar, I picked it up and dragged it with me. There was no way I was giving up my seat. I ordered a cider. It was my first taste of Kopparberg Pear cider, which became my go to drink the entire trip. Smooth, sweet, delicious. Surely, a couple of these would help my sore muscles. The band was good, really good for a Scottish band playing American cover band music.

We observed two middle-aged men making the rounds. First, they stopped at the table directly in front of us, where about four twenty somethings were having a girl's night out. Looking out of place, but not deft enough to get it, they lingered. Flirting and laughing. Looking for an opening with one of the women.

When looking for a mate, the balding middle-aged male of the species snaps his wings, laughs hysterically, and dances from table to table, hoping to catch the juvenile female's eye. They congregate in a small group called a horde of desperation to exchange drinks for phone numbers.

It was fun watching the men work for attention, angling in closer, asking questions loudly, and not getting much response. It was nearly as entertaining as the band. I could tell the women were polite, but they saw these two guys as about as hot as a friends' dad.

Eventually, they set their sights a little lower, or maybe a little more realistic, and headed to our table.

"I'm Big Kev, and this is Gregor," a mountain of a man said and stuck out his hand. "Do you know the name of this song?"

"Love Shack," I answered.

"We have a winner." He smiled big, with his glasses and his thinning hair. He was a huge teddy bear of a man and looked like he loved life. His companion was a business partner who was the exact opposite—thin, dark haired, serious, and from Australia.

"What are you drinking? I'll buy you a round," he offered generously.

We put in an order and then clinked glasses. His scotch on the rocks swirled around in the glass, then he winked at me and slid a little closer.

Introductions were made. My name is unusual, so they both said it multiple times to make sure they could pronounce it correctly.

"Neen-ya," they parroted back to me, thick with their accents.

Big Kev looked down at my fingers, not even trying to attempt nonchalance. Seeing no ring there, he took it as an invitation. Getting closer, he started to lay it on thick. He was very funny, but when I brought up my boyfriend at home staying with my daughter and pulled out my phone to show him pictures and gush about him, disappointment set in.

He was a former rugby player with four gorgeous daughters and was always ready for a good time. He bought another round, and I excused myself to go to the bathroom.

While washing my hands, I found a weird little item in the vending machine. Not a condom, not a tampon, but a vibrator. Genius! Too bad I didn't have any single pounds in my pocket. I might have given it a test drive. I mean, two weeks is a long time, and a woman has *needs*. I walked back to our place at the bar and sat down. Erika was discussing her physical transformation with Big Kev.

"I eat clean, I work out, and I hike." To prove it, she flexed one arm, and both men squeezed her bicep appreciatively. Then she ran a hand down her stomach. "Core is so important."

Big Kev thought this was an invitation and also felt her abs then gave her a thumbs up and ordered her another round. I refused. I am a lightweight and very susceptible to hangovers, and I didn't want to waste a single day of this life-changing trip puking in the toilet.

"In my rugby days, I was in amazing shape, but I can still go all night. Rugby was intense, like your American football but without any pads."

If I squinted my eyes, I could see this flabby mass of masculinity in his glory days, charging onto the rugby field and then bedding his choice of women every night. He was a far cry from that peak of fitness now; middle-age came for him hard, changing his body but not his bravado.

Erika looked him up and down. "You need to be careful. You're really unhealthy. You have too much visceral fat."

"What does that mean?" he asked, dumbfounded.

"Too much visceral fat around your belly. You're a

walking heart attack." She smacked his belly with the back of her hand to prove her point.

I almost spit out my drink; literal carbonation burned up my nostrils.

To his credit, Big Kev just laughed and laughed. The man was straight up jovial, and I enjoyed that about him. You'd have thought that Big Kev and Gregor would have moved on to another table at that point, but you'd be wrong. He got a little closer and a little more handsy with Erika. She clearly was enjoying the attention in her harmless flirty way, touching hands to forearms, leaning in too close to talk because the music was so loud.

There was a lull in the conversation while we waited for the band to come back from their break, and I decided to share my fun fact from the restroom.

"Did you know there are actual *vibrators* in the vending machines in the bathrooms?" I said.

"Really?" asked Big Kev. "But if you're with me, you'd never, ever need one of those." He was winking, poking us with his elbow, and nodding his head like men do when they think their skills are top notch between the sheets.

He was getting closer and closer to us with each passing drink. The liquor seemed to give him the green light and was waving him in for a landing.

The band wrapped up, and then it was easier to talk.

Erika looked at me, exhausted. "Are you ready to go?"

It was music to my ears. I was ready twenty minutes ago.

Big Kev looked crushed. "Before you go, let me give you my number. We will be here one more day. Let's get together tomorrow night."

Erika took his number like any good girl would who's already consumed nearly twenty pounds worth of a man's drinks, and we left.

Walking home was eerie. So quiet in this ancient city. Not many people on the roads.

"I can see why Jack the Ripper was never caught. It's so dark here, and there are no witnesses," I said.

Erika laughed and led us home. She had a great sense of direction, and I have always been an amazing follower.

TWENTY-TWO

Our final day in Edinburgh, we woke to the sound of a street performer playing bagpipes. I smiled. Still in Scotland. Bagpipes have that distinctive melancholy, haunting sound that is like nothing else. The only time I heard bagpipes was in Edinburgh from a man dressed in a full formal kilt, fully accessorized with the man purse to hide his flask and white boots with the tiny black buttons racing up the sides. I know he did it for the tourists, but still, it was incredibly charming.

Now nearly a professional at making instant coffee, we packed up and planned our day. First a little shopping, and then a ghost comedy tour on a double decker bus. One more thing I could cross off my bucket list.

We bought tickets and walked to the pick-up point, arriving about seven minutes before the start of the tour. Seeing no people and, most importantly, no bus, we started to panic that we weren't in the right location. We stopped people walking the opposite way on the sidewalk to ask for directions. Erika's loud, "Excuse me," got attention. She walked right up to people, saying it over and over until we found someone who answered us.

"That's actually up there." An elderly man turned and pointed to the bridge five blocks away on the top of a huge hill.

"Oh shit. We need to run," Erika said, and she took off, running down the sidewalks of Edinburgh, dodging the throngs of people going the opposite direction. I ran after her, trying to keep up, but after three blocks, I crouched down. Stomach cramps, ragged breath, I was pretty sure the end was near.

Erika was stopped a block away, waiting for me to catch up. I pushed on and ran to her and then crouched down again, breathing fast.

"Save yourself," I said, waving her on and still trying to catch my breath.

"Get up, Ninya. We've got to run to make it. You can do it."

So, I sucked it up, holding my side to diffuse the pain of the ache, and we ran and ran until we got to a staircase. I froze at the bottom, stunned when I realized we still had to climb up six stories of stone staircases.

"Oh, God," I cried, but I pushed myself, calves screaming. Up and up and up. My heart pounded in my chest. "This is how it ends."

"I'm going ahead," Erika called over her shoulder. "I'll make them wait for you." She disappeared into the crowd. I focused on the words *non-refundable tickets,* found the last bit of resolve deep within my soul that lived next to my inner cheapskate and ran. Heart clamoring in my chest, completely out of breath, finally, I made it to the top of the staircase with only one more block to run. Seeing the bus still parked on the curb, I relaxed and finally ran the last block, finding Erika next to the fence. I squatted down to catch my breath.

Our tour guide was a young Scot dressed like the brother of Beetlejuice, complete with a bad dental prosthetic that made him slur his words slightly. Slightly humpbacked, wearing a top hat and black tuxedo tails, in full makeup, he was a crazy looking character. He was standing outside the entrance to the double decker black bus that was leaking smoke machine fog onto the pavement, trying to set the spooky mood but failing miserably.

We walked up the stairs of the bus to sit on the top deck with the other tourists. Red velvet curtains and tiny lamps permanently fastened to the sides of the bus set the 1920s smoking parlor mood.

The tour began, and the bus careened down the narrow streets. Bouncing and tipping, it defied gravity. I have no idea how it remained upright while lurching through narrow streets crammed with traffic and people, but it did. The bus tour was amazing. I was getting to see parts of Edinburgh without actually having to walk. It was bliss for my tired leg muscles. We traveled through Old Town, New Town, Greyfriars Kirk, Grassmarket, and the back of Arthur's Seat. It was a relaxing way to see parts of Edinburgh without a rental car. The guide was funny and told ghost stories, and then the tour stopped at St. Cuthbert's Graveyard, one of the oldest cemeteries in all of Scotland. We got out and filed into the graveyard. Crumbling gravestones were covered in ivy and stained black and brown with mildew. Lime green moss crawled up the sides of everything. The air was filled with that faint damp, musty smell that stone gets when it's perpetually wet. We gathered around the guide, and he jumped up into a crumbling relic of a jail cell. We were in the front row so we could hear him. His accent was so thick, and I wanted to hear his words. For me, with accents, the louder the better, which meant the closer the better. We were nearly touching him as he clung to the side of an old crumbling post.

"Do you know the origin of the phrase 'dead ringer'?" He pronounced it ring-ah. "When you passed onto the afterlife, you were buried with a bell." The double 'B' words and his loose-fitting prosthetic teeth were a lethal combination. The double 'B' caused him to spit accidentally (and obviously) while he talked. A huge white glob of spit splashed down—I watched as it fell, almost in slow motion—and then landed on Erika's black jacket.

I would have ignored it to let him try to save face. Not Erika. She looked down at the wet glob in disgust and wiped it off her jacket with one abrupt and obvious flick of her wrist, shaking her head a little in repulsion. My eyes widened. I had to press my lips together to stop the laughter from escaping. The poor guy saw her do it and panicked a bit, stuttered, and then lost his focus and broke character for a second. There was a long, drawn out silence. Everyone began to get fidgety.

After a long beat, he shouted out, "Sorry!" Which sounded like a sing-song "Sore-dee."

I clamped a hand over my mouth and turned around to hide it from him. The giggles were nearly impossible to contain.

He continued down the path, and the group moved forward, engrossed in another story.

"He spit on me," she said in disgust. "Did you see that? I can't believe he spit on me."

"I know! I was dying. Your face. Sore-dee." I mimicked and then collapsed into a fit of laughter, nearly peeing myself, the event putting so much pressure on the always iffy bladder muscles of a middle-aged mother of two. "It was so funny." I laughed until my stomach hurt. "To be fair, anyone would spit with that thing in his mouth," I reasoned, trying to rationalize it.

"Sore-dee, Eh-ri-ka." I said it over and over until she started to smile.

She eventually laughed, too. It was hilarious and something we laughed about the entire trip. Even to this day, it makes me giggle.

Sore-dee, Eh-ri-ka.

The sun was setting as we walked back to the bus, and it was rare and stunning. Scotland was so cloudy while we were there, but that night, it was clear. Gorgeous orange light washed the front of the Bank of Scotland. High on a hill. The Saltire flying proudly. Edinburgh was marvelous, and we enjoyed the city, but it was the forest I craved. I couldn't wait for this part of our adventure to begin.

TWENTY-THREE

"It's an additional fifty pounds to have more than one driver on the rental car agreement, and an automatic transmission is an additional two hundred pounds," Erika explained to me in the bus on the way to Arnold Clarke to get our rental car.

I hadn't driven a manual transmission since I was seventeen, and I was terrified to drive on the other side of the road, especially when we got to the Highlands, where there were narrow one-lane roads servicing *both* directions with pull outs for alternating traffic. That type of highway seemed insane to me in a land where there are typically no shoulders and drop-offs that will kill you.

"I can do all the driving," Erika offered. "I am used to driving here anyway. I did most of the driving when I was here with my husband six months ago. Let's just save the money."

I agreed because money was tight for both of us, and to be honest, the idea of driving a tiny car down the even tinier streets made my heart palpitate. I was relieved to not have that burden.

We got off the bus and walked into Arnold Clarke with our luggage, where we waited for assistance.

"This rental is for ten days with one driver, correct?" The matronly woman behind the counter confirmed our rental with us.

Erika looked at me and winked.

"Yes, ma'am," I said.

She handed me a thick document. I saw Erika's name and address on the form. I glanced it over, noting the words, "only the licensed drivers listed here can legally drive the car." Erika was the only licensed driver listed on the document. "You are responsible for damages incurred from authorized and unauthorized drivers." It was pretty standard stuff, asking for the rights to your firstborn in order to complete the transaction.

"How will you be paying?"

I handed her my credit card.

I declined the insurance and damage protection because my credit card had both of those as perks. I was pretty proud of myself for checking into that before leaving the States.

Then we loaded up our luggage and were on our way in the tiny black Fiat they assigned us, guided by Erika's GPS that she plugged the coordinates into. I had never entered longitude and latitude to get to a location before, and it felt secret-agent otherworldly. We drove for hours, trying to leave the city, taking wrong turns occasionally and entering endless roundabouts.

I heard a loud smack, making me wince.

"Did we hit something?" I asked.

"The roads are so narrow it's bound to happen."

"What about damage to the rental car?"

"I've rented cars from Arthur Clark forever. They never look close enough when you turn them back in. I have never had a problem."

She shifted like a race car driver. I have a tendency to get car sick in situations where there is a lot of jerking and stopping. I was a little nauseous but didn't complain since she was doing her very best to get us to where we wanted to go, and I couldn't legally drive the car anyway. To be honest, I was relieved to be the passenger. Having to navigate the route on the other side of the street would have been very anxiety producing.

When you drive all over a country you don't know in a tiny car with one person, you spend a lot of time talking to them. In this case, she spent a lot of time talking about every friend and acquaintance she had and how they have wronged her. She went on and on, and I stared out the window, just taking it all in.

We shared a common career. We talked about photography and how it was dying, being completely taken over with MWACs. (Moms with a Camera). The barrier of entry into our field had been completely eliminated with the advance of technology, and the cost of owning professional grade equipment had dropped so drastically that *anyone* could afford professional grade cameras. It was getting harder and harder to eke out a living, and it was becoming a scary career to have. Erika was just as frustrated about it as I was.

She told me about her charity work with "Now I Lay Me Down to Sleep" and the parents she advocated for when the nurses weren't going to allow her in the room. I could see that, in certain situations, her brash confidence was incredibly useful. I could see that her quick decision making and in-your-face confrontational personality could actually be beneficial. She was passionate about her work and filled with compassion for couples forced to endure the birth of a stillborn baby or a baby who passed within hours of birth. The photographs she had created for these couples became the only physical memory of their sweet angel babies.

I admired her complete confidence in herself and the decisions she made. I had never met anyone with such an unwavering sense of certainty of her decisions. I was a chronic waffler and over-thinker, spending too much time ruminating in the past. She never did. It was eye-opening how much effort I was wasting with my constant self-doubt.

She spoke of her ability to speak with animals and understand them. Images of Dr. Doolittle popped into my mind. She said that animals were drawn to her farm because they instinctively knew she would help them. Having such a huge heart for animals, I discovered this was probably because animals didn't disappoint. They didn't hurt you like family did. It was a buffet of words as she talked and talked and talked. I looked out the window, enjoying the scenery and mumbling noises now and then to let her know I was listening.

"You know, I don't think I want to do photography anymore, because I hate people," Erika revealed and then laughed hysterically. I couldn't tell if she was being serious or not.

She handed me her iPad to show me her work, and it was *very* beautiful. She lived on a stunning piece of horse property, landscaped impeccably with a gorgeous greenhouse and fountain. It was every photographer's wet dream. Being near Dallas, she told me about her famous wealthy clients and her largest sale that was over five figures. It was impressive, but lately, she was struggling financially. All photographers were.

"I just neglected my business and let it die. I need to build it back up." She pulled up a photo on her phone and handed it to me. "See this boat?" It was a beautiful antique row boat.

"There is a lady in my town that copies everything I do. I got this row boat, she got one. I had access to an old rusty truck, she found one. She literally copies everything I do. I think she wants to be me."

She pulled up more photos to show me the evidence of how this woman wronged her.

"It's pathetic. I have to hide my sources and my ideas." She continued. "It's so sick. And then she saw I was doing this…" She waved her phone in my face again.

I was tired of hearing about it and said, "Nope. Stop. I don't want to see it. No more talking about a person like that. It's a waste of your time and mine." I pushed her hand away gently for emphasis.

"You're right," she agreed, putting the phone away.

That was the first time in my adult life that I'd cut someone off at the knees like that. I was not letting their poison and negativity sink into my brain any longer. It was the first time I'd set a solid boundary, and it felt amazing. I had no idea where this newfound directness came from; it honestly baffled me and was completely out of character. And the best part was I didn't have to hear another word about that woman the rest of the trip.

Our first stop with the car was Roslin to see the ruins. We got out and started walking toward the ruins, curving back further into the forest and off an old dirt path was Roslin Glen with an old armory.

"Rosslyn Chapel is beautiful, but it costs about twenty pounds each and isn't really worth it, but we can go if you want," she offered, trying to be accommodating.

"No, that's okay," I responded, wanting to be agreeable and an easy traveler.

"We can see the ruins of the armory, though, for free, and it's beautiful."

I followed her deeper in the forest, along a stream of water with an old, dilapidated bridge crumbling above us that was covered in vines. Further in, we found ruins of old buildings, the orange colored stones were nearly completely covered in ivy racing to the top. Some of the ancient brick walls were standing, some were sinking into the dirt. A forgotten place that was even more beautiful with the patina of age. The water rushed by from the nearby creek, a sound that has always relaxed me. I am most at peace by water of any kind, whether it is the ocean or a creek or a pond or just a bathtub. Water calms me like nothing else does.

We walked along a fallen tree, balancing carefully to cross a dry creek bed. It was an adventure, and I was enjoying it so much. Erika was always ahead of me, and I poked along like the annoying little brother that idolized his older brother, following him everywhere but slowing everyone down. I wasn't in a rush. I just soaked it in, marveling at everything—the ancient stonework, the little plants that grew in the cracks of stone.

Life persists. It is impossible to stop it.

I sat down on a boulder by the stream and just breathed it in. We had spent the last several days in the city, exploring Edinburgh, but this is why I came. This is what I wanted. Deep in the woods, surrounded by nature and water. This is what I instinctively knew would heal me. I sat there a long time, and Erika was really patient yet still adventurous, climbing up onto the old rickety bridge to snap photos. Then her naturally curious spirit pushed her farther ahead, looking for something to conquer. A creek to cross, a hill to climb, she was always pushing herself.

I, on the other hand, was a *sloth*.

Resting on the boulder, sunning myself like a lizard, I took off my shoes and put my feet in the cold water. I closed my eyes and listened to the rushing water. I could have stayed there for hours. The anxiety and tension were starting to unspool. It was always there for me, my fight or flight mechanism locked in the permanently on position. Cortisol coursing through me 24/7. I didn't know how to relax anymore. I didn't know how to just be with myself, how to slow down a brain that had been pickled in intense stress and fear for the last three years. The pathways of anxiety and stress became so ingrained in my brain, it was hard to see things any other way.

I wanted things to change. I wanted to be better, to let go of the generational anger and fear that paralyzed me and brought me to work with Noah in the first place, but I didn't know how.

Sitting on that boulder in the sun, I got my first taste of what I needed to do to reset myself. I left a little bit of my stress behind at the Roslin Ruins, and it felt incredible. Calmer than I'd felt in a long time, we got back in the car and drove on to Stirling Castle.

TWENTY-FOUR

S tirling Castle was set on volcanic rock and used to be a working royal residence, but today, it is an impressive site that tourists line up to see. The town of Stirling is about as charming as a town could possibly be, with the castle at the top of a series of long winding roads up the side of a mountain. Knowing we were going to be walking for a few hours, we stopped at a restaurant to grab some food before seeing the castle.

It was as Americanized food as we could find. Chicken wings, pizza, and hamburgers. It was a departure from the potato laden fried food we had eaten most of the trip.

Our food came quickly, brought by a patient Scotsman.

Erika took one look at hers and refused it. "I can't eat this. It looks freezer burnt," she said to the waiter, who was paralyzed, not knowing how to handle such a direct response. "It's disgusting."

He took her food away and comped her bill, and she announced that she would walk down to the fish and chips shop a block away and eat there.

I was fine with that and continued to eat my mediocre pizza in the peaceful silence. After about twenty minutes, we got back in the car and continued up the road to Stirling, winding up and up in circles dotted with shops and restaurants and cafes. It was adorable. The ascent took a solid ten minutes by car, and when the view opened up, we were on top of the world at the highest point of Stirling. The stone castle is set on the cliff, and it was clear why this location was strategically chosen. You could see enemies coming a mile away from any direction, so a sneak attack would never be successful. The views from Stirling Castle were 360-degrees panoramic. I couldn't wait to get out and explore my first castle in real life.

At the top of the mountain, the parking attendant stopped us.

"It's five pounds to park and twenty pounds a piece to enter," she said. Erika hesitated, trying to decide if it was worth it. I could see her weighing the benefits in her mind. She had been there before, and she didn't really need to see it again.

"Wow, that's pretty steep," she said. "It's nearly three anyway, and we would only have a couple hours to explore."

I wanted to go in, but I conceded. "No, that's okay. We can skip it."

"You can get out and look at the view, and I'll wait with the car," she offered.

"No, that's okay. The ride up here was beautiful, and I can see it from here. We can just keep going."

She looked relieved and continued to drive to our next Airbnb, but I was angry at myself for giving in. I had a habit of doing that, of not speaking up for myself and letting other people's stuff influence my decisions. I looked longingly back out the window as we started to descend the hilly cobblestone roads and felt the biggest pang of regret.

You did it again. Sacrificing what you wanted for someone else. When are you going to learn?

TWENTY-FIVE

Our next Airbnb, Erika had arranged it privately months before our trip, having stayed there with her husband on their visit several months prior. It was a converted barn stall that still smelled faintly of straw, and was tucked into a beautiful hillside. Incredibly quiet and private, it had a great view of rolling fields with mountains in the distance.

I showered and got ready for bed since we were going to get up early the next morning and go to Finnich Glen. We opted to share a bed in one of the rooms to save money. I have two sisters and was raised with a million cousins, so it didn't really bother me. Money was tight, so it was easy to make what I considered a small sacrifice.

I heard Erika's voice through the walls in the next room. I couldn't make the words out exactly, but she sounded stressed like she was having an argument with whoever was on the other end of the phone. I opened *The Outlander* on my iPad, relaxing into the story, trying to settle down before we slept, when she burst into the room.

"Oh my God, Ninya, my husband wants to kill me. My

account is overdrawn." She was talking fast and stress-eating chocolates and crackers. Pacing the room as she ate, she was clearly very distressed.

"What do you mean?" I didn't understand it at all. How does someone who owns a horse farm on an incredible property get themselves in this situation? "Can't he just transfer some money for you?"

"I'm so angry. Everything is tied up in this investment I can't get out of." She was full of nervous energy that was spilling onto me.

"There isn't anything you can do over here. Just take a shower and relax. He'll be mad, but I am sure he can handle it, and if not, then you can take care of it when you get back." I tried to reason with her.

"He's just so angry. I'm so broke. I haven't been this broke in a really long time. I mean, I have money; it's just tied up in this investment, and I can't get to it right now." She paced the room, the wood floors creaking in protest.

I tried to change the subject. "Where are we staying tomorrow?"

"What?" She shook her head. "We will figure it out. I thought we'd just play it by ear."

"You mean, we don't have a *reservation*?" I asked incredulously.

"No, we'll figure it out later."

What the fuck? We are in Scotland in May with no reservations?

I immediately pulled out my phone and started trying to download the Airbnb app. The internet connection was fighting me, making it nearly impossible since we were in such a remote area.

"I have a coupon. I'll book it," she said. Springing into action, she grabbed her phone and scrolled through the listings.

"Here's one for twenty-nine pounds."

That was *scary* cheap. Like crack den on the south side cheap.

"But there are no reviews, no photos. That's a no for me." There was no way.

"We'll have to share a bed to save money like we are here, but I'm fine with that, aren't you?" she asked, pushing me to agree.

"Yeah, I mean, I guess I'm fine with sharing. But let's keep looking."

She dug in her heels. "The owner's name is Allan. I'm sure it's fine, Ninya. Anything else in that area is over double that per night."

"Of course, it is. That is the normal going rate. This seems really sketchy to me. We might be checking in to Allan's rape apartment." In my mind, this was the plot of an episode of "Unsolved Mysteries" in the making.

"You're overreacting. I'm sure Allan is fine." She was steamrolling me, and I wasn't sure how to stop it.

"Look it up on Google Earth. Make sure there are at least some houses around there," I reasoned.

Someone we can run to, screaming for help when we escape.

"Fine, but I'm sending him a message."

"Sure, whatever." I turned back to my book.

A few minutes later, "There are other houses around," she declared. "Money is tight for me, so I say we book it. We will only be there to sleep and shower anyway."

"You can still be murdered in your sleep or in the shower. Have you learned nothing from watching *Psycho*?"

"You're being ridiculous. I'm booking it. I need your card."

I reluctantly reached in my backpack and handed her my credit card. She punched buttons fast and furious on her phone, making the reservation while we had a hint of an internet connection.

"Oh shit, Ninya. I thought it was going to ask for a credit card and give us the chance to put one it, but it charged my PayPal account. Now that's overdrawing, too, because it's connected to my bank account. I feel sick." She crossed the room, her nervous stomach making her run to the bathroom.

A few minutes later, she was back, her anxiety filling the room and rubbing off on me. "He is going to kill me. Can you transfer some money to my PayPal account so I don't have even more overdraft fees?"

I doubt that will help, but if it stops this crazy train, it's worth fifty bucks for my own sanity.

"Okay," I agreed and transferred the money, anxious to stop this reaction in her. I tried to relax again with the book.

This isn't your problem. Don't make it your problem.

"I'm going to message Allan and cancel our reservation. I'll see if he can refund it, and we can pay him in cash when we get there."

She was stressed, shoving huge pieces of chocolate croissants into her mouth then jumping up and pacing. It was hard to watch.

"I can't believe this is happening. I'm so angry right now."

Back to the book, I let her spiral. Normally, I would have made her problem mine, spending hours racking my brain for solutions to make her life easier, but I calmly said, "Look, let's just get some rest and figure it out later. There is absolutely nothing you can do about it here in Scotland."

"I know," she agreed.

Then we turned out the lights and went to sleep.

TWENTY-SIX

The alarm rang at six a.m., waking us from a deep sleep. The sun was up already, and so we got dressed and slipped downstairs to make instant coffee.

"I'm so excited for you to see Finnich Glen. You're going to love it." She was giddy with anticipation, having fully put the events of the night before behind her.

We jumped in the car, and she knew exactly how to get there without using GPS. Less than ten minutes later, we parked at a nondescript gravel lot and donned our backpacks before starting to walk. The air was clean and pure, and the pine trees were stunning, dropping handfuls of yellow needles to the rocky ground. It was cool, but I wore enough layers that I was incredibly comfortable.

I followed her, letting her get ahead of me a bit, enjoying the quiet. I savored chirps of the birds and the forest sounds, and then I heard rushing water.

She had stopped again and was waiting for me, a pile of trash to her left.

"That makes me so sad. This is private land, but people can always seem to fuck it up anyway."

I agreed, it just seemed wrong on so many levels to leave drinking straws and plastic coffee cups behind in a place as beautiful as this.

"People make me sick." She shook her head in disgust. Then she led me to a small entrance between two rock formations. "We have to climb down there." She pointed.

There was a crack leading down to the water, which you could hear but just barely see. If you didn't know it existed, you would never know it was there. If I had come here alone, I probably would have walked right past it.

Erika led the way, climbing down the slippery mud-covered rocks that were tilted at crazy angles, making the descent a little treacherous. I'm clumsy, always have been, and so I gingerly followed her, stepping where she stepped, choosing the same stones she chose. Taking my time, I occasionally clung to the massive tree roots that made up the sides of the path for balance. Then it got steeper, and there was a makeshift stone staircase with a rope handrail. I clung to it tightly, not trusting my balance or my footing on anything. The stones were muddy and damp and incredibly slippery even in my brand new hiking shoes. Half-climbing, half-sliding down the steep terrain, there was a sharp right turn, and then the view opened up. Stunningly beautiful, the water rushed in from a waterfall that was set deeper back. Orange rocks covered in lime green moss and lichen, vines and roots climbed from the soil, reaching up to the trees above. It was nearly prehistoric. Seeing an untouched natural phenomenon that had likely been there since the beginning of time was awe inspiring and almost otherworldly. I closed my eyes and reveled in it. Breathing in the scent of fresh moving water jam-packed with ions, that was so squeaky clean and like no other scent on the planet, was beyond soothing.

The best part of this? We were *alone*. We had the most

magnificent place I had ever been *completely to ourselves*. I expected something so beautiful to be crawling with tourists on a Sunday morning, but it was *all ours*. Erika walked ahead, balancing on a huge downed log. I followed her, slipping occasionally when my footing choices didn't match up with hers.

About halfway back to the waterfall, there was a rock formation called the Devil's Pulpit. This famous rock was used in an episode of *Outlander*, but to get to it, you needed to cross a pool of water.

She was ahead of me, taking off her socks and hiking shoes. "I want to re-create a photo of me on Devil's Pulpit for my website. But we need to cross here."

The rushing water filled the path, and she opted to walk across the water to the other side. I waited and watched her.

"Oh, God, it's freezing." She navigated the slippery rocks and then decided to cross at the shallowest place she could find. "Oh my God, it's so cold. I think my feet are numb." She walked quickly through the water to the other side. I took off my shoes and socks and set them next to hers, bracing for the cold. It was chilly with my shoes and socks off on *dry* land. I hesitated, knowing that when your feet get cold, you are miserable. The rock was smooth and gently ridged from centuries of water softening all the hard edges.

Grounding will reset your hormones. I heard Noah's voice in my head again and smiled.

"Oh my God, I can't feel my feet. It's so cold." She was shivering.

I looked around and saw another path to the right. If my toes could hug the bedrock, I could cross to the pulpit without getting wet at all. Judging from Erika's reaction, it was something to avoid at all costs. I could also see myself slipping and being thrust into two feet of freezing water, and

I weighed the pros and cons in my head before deciding to chance it.

Slowly hugging the wall, I curled my toes into the bedrock, trying to grip the slippery surface. I took one step and then another. I was almost to dry land, and I could see the other side. I leaned into the side of the rock, using every muscle I had to stay upright, then took a deep breath and slid my leg out as far as humanly possible and awkwardly jumped to the other side.

You'd think I had just completed a marathon. I was so proud of my accomplishment and ability to stay dry.

Taking in the view of the Devil's Pulpit and the waterfall that fed the rushing water was almost a religious experience.

This is the most magnificent sight I have ever seen.

I sat on the big boulders near the water, closed my eyes, and just soaked it up. It was a transcendent, almost spiritual moment. The water rushed and filled my ears. I didn't hear anything Erika said, but honestly, I craved the quiet. I just soaked it up. After about ten minutes, I opened my eyes and saw Erika was standing on top of the devil's pulpit. I walked over to her and pulled out my camera, watching her flex like a bodybuilder on the rock. This pose and that pose, I fired shot after shot at her.

"Raise your chin to the light."

Click. Click. Click.

She pulled off all her layers, down to just a tank top, and flexed.

It was freezing, and I have no idea how she endured that for very long. She flexed and flexed. The woman had incredible biceps. She pointed her toes and turned to the side; being a photographer, she knew how to pose her body and looked fantastic. A middle-aged woman in the best shape of her life, it was inspiring.

"Send those to me," she requested and smiled, jumping

down from the rock to the crushed gravel below. "I have to go back. My feet are freezing, they are starting to go numb."

"Mine stayed dry!" I bragged.

"That was smart. I'm going back the way you did." She pulled on her layers of clothing and started the trek back, picking her way carefully across the stones.

I stayed at the pulpit and soaked it up. This magical moment completely alone in the most beautiful place in the world was any introvert's wet dream, and I was *living* it.

This is why I am here. This is what I came to do. This is amazing.

Erika got back to her shoes and started to ascend. Fifteen minutes later, finding this enchanted place hard to leave like a lover in a warm bed, I started my trek up, finding that climbing out was slightly more challenging. On the way down, gravity makes the trip easier, but on the way up, you are using muscles you never knew existed to hoist your bodyweight up the steep rocks, using the rope as leverage.

When I got to the top, I walked to the back side of the waterfall and found Erika there, crossing the stream on rocks again. I couldn't figure out how she had gotten to the other side of the stream.

"Use the roots over there to get down," she shouted at me across the stream and pointed at them.

The drop was nearly twelve feet straight into the pond. It wasn't deep; it was just cold and wet, and I wanted to avoid cold feet at all costs. My hiking shoes were water resistant, but I didn't really want to test just *how* resistant they were.

I grabbed the branch and tried to turn around but lost my footing and rolled down the embankment, hitting a rock with my forehead. Dazed, I laid there for a second and laughed at myself. Covered in mud, bleeding from the forehead.

"Are you okay?" I heard her shout.

"Yeah, just super graceful, as usual."

I wiped the dirt and blood away and started making my way toward her, but midway through, it got deeper than I trusted myself to go. With my fresh head wound, the chances of losing my balance again were highly likely. So, I held back and watched Erika push herself further, finding long thick sticks to help navigate her balance. She was giddy and incredibly coordinated, with the adventurous spirit of a ten-year-old boy. She was fully immersed in her element, happy and curious and strong.

I took pictures and breathed the fresh air deep into my lungs, hoping that even the tiniest trace would stay with me forever. That somehow it would bind to my DNA and become part of me. This was one of my favorite places in the entire world, and seeing it, skidding down it, and bleeding on it just made it that much more real for me.

I go back to Finnich Glen in my mind over and over, re-living that moment. It was *that* breathtaking.

TWENTY-SEVEN

We loaded up the car again and headed to the Lost Valley for another hike. At lunchtime, we stopped at a little hole in the wall cafe for lunch. Smelling the bacony aroma of freshly homemade lentil soup, the sweet lady behind the counter gave us a sample before we ordered. Simple, thick, and rich, celery and carrots and tender lentils in a simmered-forever ham infused broth. I also ordered a sandwich I crave to this day—a brie, cranberry, and bacon melt. Scottish bacon is so different than our bacon in the States. It's incredibly meaty and delicious, and the gooey brie and sweet, yet tart, cranberry goodness combined in the most perfect way for an incredible grilled cheese experience. I seriously heard angels singing when I bit into it. It was that good. I still fantasize about it.

We were staying at Allan's rape apartment that night after hiking the Lost Valley, but I was a little more at ease with Allan because he humored Erika's crazy refund scheme and offer for cash, and he was very attentive and answered all our questions immediately. But I was angry that nothing else had been planned, that we had no further accommodations arranged, that we didn't even know what towns we would be visiting. It was a spontaneous journey, the kind that I never took.

Relax, she knows Scotland. It will be okay.

"The Lost Valley is so beautiful," Erika gushed as we drove down the hilly roads of the Scottish Highlands. She was ready to dive into another long hike, but I was tired. It was becoming obvious that I was not physically ready to hike my way through Scotland. The months leading up to the trip were the most difficult of my life, and I spent many days hunkered down in my apartment with Netflix and junk food. Edinburgh had worn me out, all those steps and all those stairs. Physically, I was exhausted, but it was the good kind of exhausted, and as a result, I got the best sleep there that I had gotten in the last three years. It was a refreshing change, but I didn't know if I could keep up with Erika and was starting to worry.

Finding public restrooms in Scotland had proven to be nearly impossible. We both went before we left, but I knew there would be none at the Lost Valley. There never were public bathrooms at any of the natural places we were at, and even in the towns and at the shops, there were no public restrooms of any kind. At Fort William, a kind gentleman handed us twenty-five pence required to use the one public restroom we found at the train station when he saw us nearly in tears standing in front of the ladies' room turnstile. I had never paid to pee before I went to Scotland, something I always took for granted. So, when you found one, you went, even if you didn't have to go because you never knew when you would see another.

At the Lost Valley, I groaned as I lightened my pack as much as possible and put it on, knowing the water bottle was heavy but necessary.

You'll carry it out inside you, so it will be lighter on the way down.

When we started walking, I was tired but put one foot in front of the other, giving myself an internal pep talk as I walked.

Keep going. Isn't this beautiful? Look around you. The landscape is stunning.

At first, there wasn't much to see, but then the path curved and twisted up the side of the mountain covered in baby Birch trees. White trunks and delicate leaves rustled in the wind. The first sprinkles of rain started to spit about thirty minutes into the hike. Raincoats are a must in Scotland, and my cheap Amazon find was one of the best investments I made. Erika was always far ahead of me, and I struggled to keep up. Eventually, I let her go ahead so I could just think. I could spend time inside my own head, without the barrage of words that came with being with an extrovert on a trip like this.

It was straight up for a long time, and my calves burned, and my neck ached. The pack was heavy, so I busied myself with stopping and taking photos whenever I felt I couldn't go on. There were people on the trail *running*. Running! People older than I was. I was in shock and always stepped to the side to give them clearance. The trail was narrow and ping-ponged up and down, forward and back up the mountain.

She got sick of waiting for me, but I didn't care. I couldn't keep up. She worked out every day for several hours leading up to this trip. I waited like a dumbass until two weeks before to attempt any sort of physical conditioning. The depression had me in its clutches so hard, even the prospect of the trip of a lifetime to Scotland couldn't get me out.

She kept going, higher and higher. Occasionally, she would stop at a pretty place and wait for me, huffing and puffing to catch up. Then when I did, she immediately started in again, which frustrated me so much because A: I was exhausted and needed to catch my breath, and B: the place was beautiful, and I just wanted to soak it in. But I couldn't because she wanted to keep going to the summit. She was a difficult and punishing taskmaster, her former military training and discipline kicking into high gear.

We got to a place where the boulders cascaded down the mountain, and the waterfalls were magnificent. The way the water moved and the way the boulders covered the hill made for a million tiny waterfalls all over this part of the land. It was stunning, and I took so many photos of them, picking my way across the waterfalls using the boulders as stepping stones. I felt like a fairy in a mystical world. It was so stunning, but I was tired.

We saw a family coming down.

"How much longer to the top?" I asked them.

"Just another thirty minutes. Keep going. You're almost there," they encouraged us.

My heart sank.

Erika started in again, but I just didn't have the energy to follow her.

"I can't, Erika. You go on ahead. Just go up to the summit and leave me here. When you come back down, we can continue together. I need a break."

She was annoyed.

"C'mon, Ninya. Push yourself. We are almost there."

I shook my head. "I'm so tired. I just want to sit here with my keyboard next to a waterfall and relax. You go without me."

I thought I detected an eye roll, but I couldn't be sure; I was nearly delusional with physical depletion.

"Okay, I guess I'll go."

She got up and started up the mountain again. I was relieved. I found the perfect spot and sat on a huge rock in the sun, listening to the water gushing below. I crawled around and experimented with the long exposure feature on my iPhone. I wanted to send some photos home tonight when we had an internet connection again.

I was alone with my thoughts and wanted to use this time wisely.

I am grateful I am here. It is so hard, but I am lucky I even get to have this experience.

The beautiful face of my friend Lesley popped into my mind, and my eyes filled with tears. She was a sister from the first minute we met. She loved my kids, especially my son, easily and like a mother, and she had passed away the previous July.

When things with Liam went off the rails three years ago, she was the first one to call. Everyone else disappeared like what typically occurs when a traumatic event happens. People just don't know what to do or what to say, so they vanish.

I had been crying that day for hours. It seemed surreal. I was avoiding phone calls, but when I saw her name pop up on my caller ID, I answered.

"The police found him at a park, unconscious…" I could barely say it out loud. It physically hurt to say the words. "Unconscious. Xanax," I puked out and then sobbed, keening into the phone. It hurt so much. I didn't know it then, but it was the beginning of a three-year nightmare.

"I'm so sorry this is happening. Tell me what I can do for you."

"Nothing, there is nothing anyone can do." And she listened. The story poured out, and my heart was bare. You couldn't have any defenses in Lesley's presence.

And then, several months later, she was one of five people I told about the pregnancy and the only one I confided in about considering the termination. Her cancer had come back, and any time I got to see her was precious.

She was in town buying a car with her family and asked if I could meet them at a burger joint. I drove there in pain, the hyperemesis gravidarum making me so sick I spent most of that day in front of the toilet. I was weak and depleted, but getting the news that her cancer was back made every opportunity to see her impossible to postpone. Time with her was precious and limited, so I couldn't miss this chance, no matter how terrible I physically felt. Her husband and sons were sitting at a table in the crowded restaurant, waiting for us, and I needed to tell her because I knew I might not get another chance.

Seeing my nearly green complexion and noticing I wasn't ordering any food, she said, "Are you okay?" and squeezed my arm.

A tear slid down my cheek, and I brushed it away. "Not really," I choked out.

I moved in closer and whispered the truth to her. In the middle of a burger joint, stuck in a line of people ordering their fries and shakes.

"Oh, Ninya. I can't imagine what a burden that is. I am so sorry." She put her arm around me, and I hugged her and closed my eyes. "It's official, you've earned a spot as a card-carrying member of Unluckiest Club." She smiled weakly. "So far, it was only me and one of my other friends. But with what you've gone through with Liam and this new development, you've earned full lifetime membership status." With Lesley being diagnosed with Marfan Syndrome and then fighting cancer twice, it was brutal company to be among.

"I never thought I was capable of having an abortion. But I just don't think I can do it. I have nothing left to give this baby, and Josie and Liam would suffer even more," I whispered as I wiped away the tears with my fingers in the packed restaurant.

"That's just impossible, an impossible situation, and no one can fault you for the way you feel. No judgement from me. Whatever you decide is the right decision." She hugged me tight, and I felt heard and a little less ashamed.

It was the last one-on-one conversation we ever had. A few months later, cancer stole her from us. She was the most loving and accepting human being I had ever met. She held space for me in a way I have never experienced before and to this day have not found in another human being. She loved Liam, and she loved me, and she is someone I think about all the time. I wish we had gotten more time with her and her family. At her funeral, the standing room only service showed me how much she was loved and how many people she brought this kind of beautiful peace and acceptance to. Knowing her was such a gift.

It is a privilege to be alive, to be here, and to get to have an experience like this. Lesley didn't get that chance. Don't waste it.

The rain started to fall gently and hid my tears, washing them away, then after ten more minutes, the sun came out again. Scotland in May is like that couple who is fighting one second and then fucking the next. So unpredictable, and you have to be prepared, with rain coats at the ready for the makeup sex. It's the same in Scotland.

I peeled off my shoes and socks, placed my feet on the rocks, and crawled between boulders, finding the perfect place to set up my makeshift laptop. Next to a family of waterfalls, I wrote about what was happening and our days here. Little did I know that those words would become the basis of this book. I was just journaling like I always have, processing my experiences through words, finding myself a little less lost in the Lost Valley.

Forty-five minutes later, she descended and caught back up with me.

"You missed it. It was beautiful," she gushed, flushed pink with effort.

"I didn't miss anything. It was beautiful here, too."

She once again led the way, and I followed her back to the car so we could get to Allan's rape apartment.

TWENTY-EIGHT

Allan's rape apartment was cheap but turned out to be really safe. And Allan turned out to be an incredibly sweet and gentle elderly man, whose grandson had talked him into supplementing his income using Airbnb. We were his very first guests. In the tiny mountain town of Kinlochleven, pocket-sized white and red cottages complete with flower boxes framed the gigantic mountains behind. It was a tiny, quiet town with a river that ran through it, powering a massive water wheel. It was the epitome of adorable, and so was Allan.

He offered to carry our luggage upstairs, but he was so frail, I wasn't totally sure he'd make it to the top. A bus driver by trade, we pumped him for information, or I should say, Erika pumped him for information because I was exhausted after our long physical day and ready for food and then sleep. In the true klutz-master fashion that I am famous for, I managed to trip on rocks on the path in the Lost Valley, and landed on my back again, laughing into the aspen trees. I thought I might have pulled a back muscle.

I organized my things in the small postage stamp of a

room, so small you had to almost scoot across the bed to get to the other side of it. Erika was first in the room, and I was starting to see a pattern of her always claiming the best spot for herself, the one with the only table and best access to the outlets. I am pretty passive, and so I just lived with it and didn't put up a fight because it just wasn't worth it. But I noticed and kept score in the quiet, passive aggressive way that I hate myself for doing but continue to do anyway. Then she walked into Allan's living room like she owned the place and struck up a conversation with him about everything.

She made herself at home in Allan's small and shabby living room that was covered in shelves with hundreds of exquisitely carved dragon figurines with colored crystals for eyes. The contrast of these detailed statues and his humble apartment was humorously incongruent. It was obvious to anyone with eyes where the majority of his salary was going. He gave us the Wi-Fi password, and I listened to him talk to Erika with his thick Scottish brogue—a lilting language full of fun words like wee, bairn, and eejit, which I discovered means idiot. Having a massive crush on Gerard Butler from nearly birth, I have always loved a Scottish accent. I could tell he just wanted to watch his TV programs, but he was too polite and accommodating, so he was forced to endure Erika's endless litany of questions. He answered them all. Allan was a saint.

Finally, she got to the most important one.

"Where's the best fish and chips?" She drilled him.

He gave her two options, both within walking distance. Yay. Food. I was nearly salivating at the prospect.

Erika was ready to sit at the pub for hours, chatting it up with the locals, and all I wanted to do was eat and then sleep.

The Harry Potter train wasn't far from there, and I tried to buy tickets online because I had never traveled by train and thought, why not? When would I ever get another chance to do this? To be honest, I was mostly motivated by not having to hike for the day, ready to just ride on my ass because everything was so sore. Muscles I didn't even know existed were angry. I needed a break, and Erika seemed to be excited to try it as well because it was something she had never done during all her trips to Scotland. My spirits were a little dashed when I discovered it had been sold out for months. Steeling myself for another hike the next day, we walked to the pub for dinner.

I was learning that Scottish pubs usually didn't have wait staff. You bellied up to the bar to order drinks *and* food. So, we did that and ordered fish and chips. Again. No regrets. I ordered another pear cider. It was my go-to drink the entire trip, and I mourn the loss of it now that I am home and can't find it anywhere. Then we settled into a table to wait for our food.

Erika was on a roll. Her fish and chips eating streak that started the first day had continued for the first week, daily, maybe even twice a day sometimes. I liked to try other things and didn't usually join in her obsession, but this pub had a very limited menu.

The food arrived at our table, and the waiter set identical plates in front of us. Erika took one look at hers and said, "Your piece is so much bigger than mine," pouting and judging. I looked down at the plates. It wasn't.

"Do you want to trade?" I asked, trying to placate her, knowing I probably wasn't going to eat it all anyway.

"No, this is fine," she mumbled, and we ate in silence. I gobbled up the mashed peas and left some chips on my plate, peeling the batter off the fish and dipping it in copious amounts of tartar, to the dismay of the bar staff who had to bring us much more than normal people require. I watched the staff deliver plate after plate of food to hungry diners that nearly always included chips. Scotland was the land of carbs, and chips came with *everything*, literally everything. Mac and cheese and chips, quiche and chips, pasta and chips. Double carbs were the norm. Completely stuffed and ready to shower and sleep, we left the pub and started walking back to Allan's.

"Come have one more drink with me," Erika begged. "I'm not ready to go to bed yet."

I just wanted a book and bed, but I was trying to be agreeable. "One drink," I reluctantly agreed. I was having a hard time reconciling in my mind this person, freaking out about finances to the point that we were staying in sketchy places and sharing a bed, yet wanting to go to the pub every night and drink for hours. I didn't have the money to do that, and according to what she was telling me, she didn't either.

We walked into another pub and ordered more cider, talking about how disappointed we were about the train. I finished my drink pretty quickly and said, "Girl, I'm exhausted. I'm going back to read and sleep."

"Fine. Leave me here at the pub." She pouted.

"You make friends wherever you go. You'll be fine." It was the truth, and to be honest, I wished I had a little of that skill in me. Plagued by social anxiety, it usually held me back in social situations. For years, I always hated my introvert ways and saw them as a weakness, but I was learning that there was nothing wrong with me and nothing that had to be fixed. It was just who I was, and that was okay.

Erika was unencumbered by that and loved to talk to people in Scotland. She fed off of it, actually. Normally, the guilt trip she was laying on would have made me stay and begrudgingly keep her company, waiting for her to decide when it was time for us to go home. But a tiny seed of independence and confidence was starting to grow. I spoke up for myself for the first time instead of pushing my own needs down. It was a brand-new feeling for me.

Feeling like a conqueror with my newfound ability to advocate for myself, I walked home, savoring the quiet and soaking up the sights of this little jewel of a town tucked into the mountains. At Allan's, I gathered my things to take a shower in the only bathroom in the house. The towels provided were like sandpaper, having air dried on a tiny rope cord hanging in the bathroom since dryers are not standard in every home in Scotland. There was hair in the drain and a canister of shaving cream on the tiny sink. Scotland is also the land of plumbing fixtures made for little people. The ancient claw faucet groaned when I turned it on to brush my teeth. A cracked mirror with harsh overhead lighting that turned on with a long, threaded cord was in the corner of the room. But the shower was relatively clean, and the water was relatively hot, and that was good enough for me.

I finished quickly and got a text from Erika on WhatsApp.

Erika: There is another train. And it's cheap. I was chatting up the bartender, and the locals told me about it. It is the regular train that goes to Mallaig. Exact same route, half the cost, and you don't need a reservation.
Me: Awesome. Let's do it tomorrow.

Her outgoing social butterfly interactions with the pub patrons had found us a solution. She came home excited a few hours later, filled with pride that her extroverted ways had earned us a ride on the train after all. I was excited about it, too, since resting my sore legs for a day and letting the train do the work sounded like heaven.

"See? This is why I talk to the locals. We would have never known about the train if I wasn't sitting in that pub." She was really happy with herself.

"Yeah, that's awesome," I agreed. The best part of that whole scenario was, I didn't have to be there.

She crawled into bed next to me, and we both fell asleep.

In the middle of the night, I heard the most awful retching sounds through the paper-thin walls of Allan's apartment. Puking for hours. It was Erika. The fish and chips were fighting their way out. Over and over, she vomited. At one point, I considered knocking on the door to see if she was okay but then fell back asleep. I have to admit, it was a little poetic justice to me, and the irony made me smirk because, clearly, I am a terrible person.

I eat clean, Ninya. Mostly veggies and free-range eggs.

Her mantra had been drilled into my head. I'd heard it from her a million times.

The next morning, Allan left us alone in his house as he went to work his early bus driving shift. Kinlochleven wasn't the kind of town where you locked your doors. Blind trust was built into the water supply that the water wheel cranked into each home every day. It was refreshing. There aren't many places in the world where you can say that anymore. We packed our bags up and left, headed for our train adventure on the Harry Potter bridge.

TWENTY-NINE

I had never been on a train. We parked the rental car at Fort William, and I bought the tickets. More charges on my credit card, more expenses she couldn't pay with cash. They were starting to add up, but I pushed away that thought, knowing there was nothing else I could do. Then we waited for the train to Mallaig.

The journey would take an hour, and I wanted to write, so I chose a seat away from Erika with an outlet and pulled out my keyboard and started in. It felt so decadent and cosmopolitan to be on a train in the UK, pumping out my word count. I was journaling so I could blog about the trip. The social media fast was actually quieting my mind and opening up my time. Coupled with no Netflix and having to rely on only writing and books for entertainment, it was starting to calm my primordial brain. The go-go-go was being replaced with space for quieter reflection. Traveling in Europe is something I had always romanticized in my mind. Being there was different and took a bit of an adjustment. But when you finally do, when you finally relax and exhale and know that you don't have to always rush through things, it is so good. There wasn't this need and desire to force myself through things as fast as possible to get on to the next thing on my agenda. There were no appointments to go to, no deadlines to meet. I had time freedom there like I never experienced since before the birth of my children.

As the landscape rushed by us on the train, I wrote,

I will return stronger, physically and mentally. I traveled to Europe with only a carry-on, and I truly had everything I needed and nothing I didn't. We are over ⅓ of the way through our trip, and things are slowing down. I am feeling more capable and confident, able to enjoy what is in front of me, even if I am frustrated. I have learned that I can choose to take anything I want from any experience. It is not dependent on who I am with. It comes from within me.

Erika sat next to me, surfing the internet, scrolling through social media, texting her husband, and taking photos. She was quieter, too. I'm not sure if she was still queasy from the fish and chips episode at Allan's or something else.

We got off the train an hour later at Mallaig, a tiny picturesque fishing village. The sky was so blue, and the seagulls were very friendly, swooping in and back down again. I played with the time lapse feature on my iPhone, snapping live photos of them flying down in front of a mural.

We walked and walked and were hungry again. There were only a couple of options in this tiny town. We saw a restaurant filled with people out on the patio, which usually is the tell of something good, so I followed her into it.

She strode with purpose right up to the hostess station.

"Excuse me," she blurted a little too loudly. "How long is the wait?" she demanded.

The hostess looked us over cooly and then met her directness and said, "I can seat you now." She grabbed two menus and tried to seat us next to the door.

Erika saw another table by the window that was open and asked, "Can we have that one?"

"No," she decided firmly. "You can have *this* table." Then she set the menus on the table. I pulled out a chair, getting ready to sit down.

Erika refused, immediately irritated. "But no one is sitting there."

"That is already reserved for another party." The hostess continued to spar with her.

"No, thank you," she replied and stormed out of the place, shaking her head. I followed her, quietly mumbling a, "Sorry," that I don't think the hostess heard.

Erika was outraged and walked faster, looking for another option in a tiny town crawling with hungry tourists. "Did you hear how she spoke to me? What a bitch! What was wrong with giving us that table?"

She's just reflecting back the energy you were giving to her and setting her boundaries.

Erika seemed to love her own boundaries, but others' boundaries, not so much.

I followed her down another road, and she walked right into a beautiful postage stamp of a restaurant with huge windows, crisp white table cloths, and amazing views to the sea.

She was still frustrated and ordered her Cullen skink, another Scotch delicacy that I grew to love, and an appetizer of fresh langoustines. Cullen skink is a creamy fish chowder with potatoes, cream, and cod. I ordered the salmon with pepper relish and vegetables. Salmon is not normally something I look forward to or ever enjoy. It is normally something I force myself to eat in an attempt to be healthier, but I had to give it a chance where it was fresh and local.

Her food came first, and she gobbled it up in front of me.

"There is a weird smokiness I don't like." She ate with a frown. Starving, I looked at the bread longingly, but it was on her side of the table and came with the soup. It didn't feel right eating it, and she never offered, so I waited.

"This bowl is half empty," she whined while she spooned it into her mouth. Her langoustines that looked like giant shrimp, eyes fully intact, arrived next. She ripped a head off and took a bite of one.

"These aren't very good either," she complained. "This is the most we have spent at a restaurant the whole trip, and it wasn't even worth it. I'm so disappointed."

I watched her eat quietly. I was starving. My meal came out eventually and was a revelation. Salmon so fresh, the gorgeous pink meat contrasting with the green relish. I don't really know what umami means, but I think if ever a flavor combination had it, this was it. Everything popped in my mouth. The fresh, cracked peppery crust was beautiful and spicy, and the cucumber relish was an explosion of flavors, crunchy, sweet, and savory at the same time. The veggies were so fresh they tasted like they were picked that morning. Green pea pods and cooked carrots, soft creamy boiled new potatoes. I was in heaven. It was the most amazing meal, and I savored it slowly.

She watched me, and I was careful not to tell her more than once how good it was until all the salmon was gone because I knew I'd see her fork break the plane of decency and she'd help herself to a bite. It was so good, I couldn't bring myself to share the salmon, but I did offer her a taste of the relish and to help me with the vegetables. I'm not a monster.

Full and happy, we walked around the beautiful port of Mallaig. Red fishing boats lined the docks, and puffy white clouds dotted the saturated blue sky. High on the hill, across the expanse of water, cottages lined the landscape. It was another postcard. We caught the train back to Fort William, and that is where the money shot could be found. The iconic Harry Potter Hogwarts train on the aqueduct. We jumped up to take the photo, and as the train passed, I saw dots of people in the valley below taking photos from their angle.

I opened my phone and saw a snapchat notification. I never really understood or loved snapchat except for one feature, the filters for videos. Ryan had taken to recording videos with the hotdog filter that made his voice sound like one of the Chipmunks and they were so cute.

I pressed play, smiling down at the video of his perfect white teeth and giant brown eyes superimposed on a hotdog in a bun, and the pang of missing him hit my heart. "Here's a wiener video all the way from the United States to Scotland. Hope you sleep well, sweetheart." He always made me giggle, and I missed home so much.

THIRTY

"How are things going?" The international phone that Ryan had set up for me was a lifeline home. We had been able to text, but there is nothing like hearing the voice of someone you love when you are so physically far away from them.

"Good, I think," he reported in the relaxed, easy way he does. "She's staying with Megan mostly, but Emily and I are in contact to make sure her rides are covered and she is getting everywhere she needs to be."

"You have no idea how much I appreciate this."

"I think I do. Are you having a good time?"

"Well..." I hesitated. "Yes. I am, but it's not the trip I signed up for. She wants to go-go-go, and I want to sit and take breaks and marvel at the beauty. We've been butting heads a little. She's a strong personality."

"Just advocate for yourself." He paused. "Someone is dying to talk to you."

"Mommy!" Her sweet voice filled the space between us, making my heart crack wide open. She only called me that ironically, but it was still music to my ears.

"So, what's happening? Tell me everything. Leave nothing out," I begged.

"Nothing is happening. Just school and work. But we started the Sex Ed Unit in health class."

"Did you now?" I teased her.

"And one of the assignments is to interview a parent about their first experience and what they thought about it."

"Wow, okay." That was going to be hard since the only functioning parent was over three thousand miles away.

"It's so awkward, Mom. I don't want to talk about this stuff with adults."

"I know, honey. But Megan and Emily are girls. They will go easy on you."

"Nah, I think I'll interview Ryan."

I was shocked.

"Umm, really? You wouldn't feel uncomfortable?"

"I know him a lot better than Megan and Emily. It will be fine."

Dear lord. Ryan will want to die.

Being a career bachelor, I am sure he certainly never anticipated the need to have a frank discussion about sex with a fourteen-year-old when he offered to help take care of my daughter.

We chatted a bit more. "Okay, girl, I am tired and need to go. I love you. Let me say goodbye to Ryan."

"Hey, babe." His voice filled my ears again, making me long for home and yearn to be snuggled up to his nice warm body. The man radiated heat, and I often tell him that's the only reason we're together since I am perpetually cold.

"So, I have something to talk to you about. Josie needs to have a discussion with an adult about sex for her health class."

"Oh, God." He was stunned.

"I know, honey. It's a lot to ask. Probably your worst

nightmare come true. But when I told her to talk to Emily or Megan, she said she'd rather talk to you."

"What in the actual fuck?" I could hear a little panic in his voice.

"I can try and reach the teacher by email and see if it can be postponed until I get back."

He sighed. "No. I'll do it."

"You don't have to. I am sure we can get an extension."

"No, I can get through one awkward conversation with your daughter. I don't want you to worry or have to take care of anything while you are there."

"Ah, babe, you're the best! I seriously hit the jackpot with you. I'll make it up to you when I get home."

"You better!" He laughed again.

"It's so good to hear your voice. I miss you."

"I miss you, too, babe. Goodnight."

THIRTY-ONE

In the morning, we entered the Isle of Skye on the GPS, and a little over an hour later, we found ourselves accidentally back in Mallaig. The shortest route required us to board the ferry with our rental car to get to the Isle of Skye. It was a gamble since we hadn't purchased a ticket in advance. We were directed to the standby lanes, begging our way onto the ferry, which was quite a feat because it was the beginning of the tourist season. May is a popular time to visit Scotland because the midges aren't out yet. The midges were spawn of the devil, tiny little biting insects that made wearing those netted mosquito hats both fashionable and functional. We sat in line, silently begging and praying for a spot to be open for us on the ferry, and were greatly relieved when we were waved onto the ship.

On the boat, Erika saw a dog owner roughly grab his dog by the scruff of his neck and was instantly incensed. Incredibly irate, she shook with bottled rage. I don't like the mistreatment of animals either, but she was fanatical about it.

"I don't see the big deal. I mean, that's how their mother's do it," I reasoned.

She shook her head. "It's cruel." Then she stalked off and into the cabin to befriend yet another dog, leaving me on the top deck.

I caught a glimpse of a seal, the first one I had ever seen in the wild. A shiny flash of black rubbery skin, and then he jumped from the nearly black rocks to the water. It was beautiful. I sat on the deck, enjoying the quiet, but then got a little cold so I found shelter and Erika. She was deep in a conversation with a couple about their dog and her dog, and how much she missed him and her farm, and how her horses pouted when she was gone and refused to eat. A story I had heard nearly twelve million times already. The journey on the ferry was short, and then we got back in our car and drove onto the Isle of Skye.

Breathtaking views were literally everywhere. Black craggy rocks, with white surf beating itself into them again and again. Bright greens and yellow hedges covered in flowers. Everywhere you looked was a photograph. She drove us to the Quirang, at the top of the mountain, driving on twisty one lane roads that serviced *both* directions, having to stop for sheep to cross many times.

The parking lot was makeshift, just a pile of gravel where a tour bus was haphazardly parked, with not a single public bathroom to be found. I was mentally calculating how much water I could drink and not have to pee on the trail, and at the same time, not become dehydrated. I have a shy bladder, and peeing in public has always been a nearly impossible task for me, made even harder because, on the Quirang, there are few trees to hide behind.

But the impending bladder pain was worth it. The view was easily the most beautiful in all of Scotland. Rock formations framed the sea. The ocean revealed itself in a display of mixed navy and teal blue colors like I had never seen before. Dark brown rocks laid siege while white surf pounded the rocks. The tide washed in and out like a heartbeat. It was spectacular.

I pulled on my pack, which was still heavy. Over the last few days, it had gotten better as I had grown physically stronger, but carrying it for any long length of time was still uncomfortable.

Erika smiled. She was in her element. "Let's go." She picked her way down the one-way path. It was literally fourteen inches wide and weaved in and out of the rocky terrain. She climbed higher and was faster than I was. About a mile in, the path became more treacherous, with drop-offs that went straight down. If I tripped, which I had to admit was incredibly likely, I'd be rolling down the mountain like Westley on *Princess Bride*. I was terrified. Leaning to the left, clinging to the mountain, I picked my way down the path as Erika disappeared.

I finally came around the bend and found Erika, talking with a man, taking photos, sitting in the deep grass on the side of the mountain facing the ocean.

Yes! Finally, I will get to catch my breath, maybe pull out my keyboard and write.

She wrapped up her conversation the second I arrived and was ready for us to press on.

"Let me just catch my breath. It's so beautiful here." I pulled my backpack off and set it on the grassy side of the mountain.

Sitting down, I took out the water bottle and sipped it, looking at my keyboard longingly, but knowing if I pulled it out there would be an argument.

This is what you came to do. Relax and replenish.

"Why don't you go on without me, and then on the way

back, you can meet up with me here, and we can walk to the car?"

"This trail is a circle. It's not the same route."

Um. It can be. You could hike for an hour in one direction and then turn around and come back for me.

I begrudgingly gathered up my stuff and groaned as the pack slipped on my sore shoulders.

She started up the mountain again, and this time I didn't force myself to try to keep up. I was scared. Gravel made the trail even more treacherous. I couldn't see her anymore.

I hurt. I was terrified. I just wanted to sit on the mountain and rest, and I was getting angry about it.

Stop it. You have no right to complain about this, about being here in Scotland. Lesley never got to see this. Your mom never got to see this. You are being a selfish baby.

I walked alone on the narrow, perilous trail, engrossed in my own thoughts. Having all that time to think was equal parts good and bad. I had come here to heal myself, and the most painful thing I'd ever endured had happened the previous October and had left the deepest scars. Until Scotland, I just used Band-aids on the bullet wound, but I had come to Scotland to heal myself. The trip would have been a failure if I didn't tackle that.

THIRTY-TWO

In October, I downloaded Plenty of Fish. I put up a profile to dip my toe in the dating pool again, and one night stumbled across Ryan's profile. He was funny and nerdy and had gorgeous brown eyes and an amazing smile. People our age on these apps have battle scars. It's easy to tell who hates life and has been beaten down because the evidence is written all over our faces.

He was different. Easy to talk to, worked out, made me laugh. We began a fun night of texts back and forth, and it was highly entertaining.

Then one text message interrupted our flirty first night of banter, and it was a sucker punch. So extreme and paralyzing, something I never dreamed would happen in a million years.

A group text, including Josie, Liam, Jack, Cal, and myself popped up with the words:

Cal: Thought you should know. Your mother murdered your brother or sister.

He sent those eleven hateful words in a *group text* to my children and his own son.

Those words burned everything to the ground. Cal had become a monster so desperate to hurt me at any cost, that he didn't care who he victimized. Willing to use my clinically depressed children and willing to reveal something this devastating in the most callous way to his *own* son, not fathoming for a second how it would hurt the kids. His lust for revenge and hatred of me outweighed everything else. His only goal was my total destruction and this was the fastest way to ensure it.

My daughter had blocked Cal previously, so she didn't receive the group text. Since Liam knew, it was only a matter of time before he would make it his duty to inform her of what I had done. The last three years had turned our relationship into a battleground and all our interactions had turned into hostile attacks that left many deep scars.

I panicked and couldn't breathe. Time morphed and slowed down until it was almost an out of body experience, the trauma forcing my brain to separate from my body to offer a layer of protection. Fighting for survival by numbing me. I was stuck in a silent slow-motion vacuum waiting for the next bomb to hit, unable to put a single thought together.

Immediately, my son texted me. Over and over, a hateful litany of messages that I deserved.

Liam: Fuck you, Ninya. Don't fucking talk to me like we are ever going to have a relationship.

You're such a two-faced person. I know you were never going to tell me or any of us, and I want you to know you are a fucking scumbag and such a shitty person for doing this.

**How can you expect me to tell the truth and be
this fucking angel when you won't even do the
same? Fuck you! I'm done, Ninya. 100% fucking
done.**

**After all the shit I've had to do because you didn't
agree with it. Because it wasn't your fucking perfect
lifestyle of holy Christian bullshit.**

**FUCK YOU. FUCK GOD. FUCK ALL YOUR BULL-
SHIT CAUSE YOU'E JUST AS FUCKING BAD AS
ME, YOU LYING FUCK. YOU HOLD EVERYONE
TO SOME FUCKING STANDARD YOU WON'T
EVEN HOLD YOURSELF TO. DON'T EVER
LECTURE ME AGAIN ON FUCKING MORALS
AND WHAT'S THE RIGHT THING TO DO
BECAUSE YOU HAVE NO ROOM TO TALK.
MAYBE THIS WILL MAKE YOU REALIZE YOU'RE
A FUCKING SHIT PARENT.**

He lashed out. Each text was a bullet, and I felt them all. It was a pain that was so excruciating, I was hyperventilating reading his messages.

Seconds later, my Facebook notifications started blowing up.

Stunned, I opened Facebook on my computer to see that Liam had posted a screenshot of Cal's vicious message along with his commentary about my substandard parenting skills. Liam had taken to social media to expose me, knowing this was how I made my living, knowing it was the death blow to my career. Of all the ways he could inflict pain, Liam knew this one would hurt the most.

My brother called. He was upset, disappointed in me, and didn't understand how I could have done it.

156

"You need to stay away from men," he lectured, and I felt his judgment.

When he hung up, we didn't speak for a year.

I called my sister, who knew I was pregnant and had called me fertile myrtle just a few weeks prior. She heard the pain in my voice and replied, "I just wish you had told me the truth. I don't agree with your decision, but I love you anyway." Shame filled me. There was nowhere to hide. My deepest sin had been exposed publicly. I had never felt pain like this.

I made calls to the few people who knew I was pregnant, so they would hear it from me before seeing Liam's Facebook page. They were the most painful phone calls I have ever made. Months prior, I had told them all that I started to bleed and that the baby was gone. It wasn't the complete truth, but I hadn't wanted to lie to them either. I know I was mincing words, and that it was still wrong. Now, I had to tell them that I terminated the pregnancy, that it wasn't the miscarriage they all had concluded it to be.

Then I steeled the little resources I had left to tell my then thirteen-year-old daughter. I walked to her room, heavy with the secret, knowing I had little time before my son exposed my sins to her.

Eyes red and shaking, I struggled to find the right words to tell her. I braced for her judgement and her anger, and I started in. "Honey, I need to tell you something." And it all came out. She listened quietly, and her response shocked me.

She walked to me with open arms and held and hugged me tightly. I clung to her thin frame, ashamed that my daughter was comforting me, but needing support so badly from someone who loved me.

"I am so proud of you for making a decision that was right for you when it goes against everything you believe in. I know how hard that was for you." She cried as she held me, her little body shaking with mine, but her words were strong. "I love you so much, Mom. You are the strongest person I know, and even if this makes us have to move into an even crappier apartment, it's okay because we will still be together. You have been there for me my whole life. I love you so much."

I sobbed and sobbed with relief and shock that the biggest comfort came from my sweet teenage daughter. I expected her to be disappointed in me. I expected her to hate me for what I had done, but she came at me with such love that it broke my heart.

I drove to the police station to see if I could file a report against Cal for harassment of my children. I waited for the officer, glancing at my phone. It had been lighting up all night with messages from Ryan, and I thought, *I am a train wreck. This is not the right time. I am a mess.* In the waiting room, I finally messaged him back.

Me: Something terrible happened with my children. I am at the police station waiting to file a report.
Ryan: Oh no. I hope everything is okay. Message me when you get home so I know you're okay.

This was typical Ryan. To this day, he asks me to message him when I get home, whether it's just going from his house to my apartment or somewhere out of state. He cared about my well-being from the beginning and still does. That is what a solid, healthy man does, and I wasn't used to it at all.

THIRTY-THREE

Still on the Quirang, having to pee but not having enough cover to do it was stress-inducing. I walked quietly down the track that was built for mountain goats. The sides of the steep trail we were on were dotted with sheep and lambs, all looking more at ease and confident on the difficult terrain than I was.

I was tired. The pack dug into my shoulders, and the arthritis in my neck was screaming. This entire trip was punishing to my calf muscles, weak from atrophy from lying in bed, eating junk, and numbing my brain with Netflix until I was distracted enough to sleep. I was not physically prepared to take on a trip of this magnitude. In contrast, Erika had spent hours at the gym lifting weights and was taking long hikes on the weekends for hours with her husband leading up to this. I remember messaging her in a panic when it was only a few weeks out.

Me: I've been so depressed. Hard to get out of bed. I don't think I'm physically ready for all this hiking.

Erika: Don't worry about it. We are going to have so much fun. If you need to rest, we will.

But Erika was like the ever-elusive carrot. Just out of reach, always ahead, and I strained to keep up. My heart was clamoring out of my chest. She would get ahead of me, then wait for me to catch up, and then immediately leave again while I sucked in air and rested, and then she'd wait again. It was a frustrating cat and mouse game I was playing, trying to keep up with her. So, I just stopped trying to keep up. When I was tired, I took a break and snapped a few photos. I drank some water, and I scoured the bare terrain for a secret place to pee, never finding it. I could tell she was frustrated.

She'd say things like, "Keep going. Isn't this amazing?"

My least favorite was when she said, "You have to push yourself. When I came here with my niece last year, she was a trooper. Made it to the top, never complaining, and she has fifty pounds on you."

I didn't like the comparison. It irritated me. Eventually, we came to a fence with a staircase that was boxed in.

Finally, we can turn back now.

She proceeded to hop the fence and continued hiking.

"Are you sure we are supposed to do this?" I asked. "Seems like they went to great lengths to keep people out of this part."

"It's to keep the sheep out. Just jump the fence."

"I can't, Erika. I am too tired. Go ahead without me."

"But I won't be coming back this way."

"But you can *choose* to come back this way *for me*."

She shook her head, annoyed at my weakness and that I was giving up too easily.

"I'm exhausted and scared to death. This has been the scariest hike we have ever been on. It's literally straight down, and I will be rolling down the Quirang to my death if I trip. We've both seen what I am capable of at Finnich Glen."

"So, you want to go back?"

I nodded, yes.

"Fine. But you know you'll never break through if you don't push yourself."

"I didn't come here to push myself. I came here to heal and replenish."

"Fine, then we'll head back," she said dismissively and turned and walked ahead, picking up her pace again like she was part mountain goat. I stayed behind, lost in my own thoughts. Consumed with picking the exact right place to put my foot next that wouldn't send me tumbling down the mountain; it was amazing how much of my brain power that one task consumed.

She waited by the car for me at the end. I smiled, and we jumped in.

"I think we want different things from this trip," I began. "You want to go and push yourself, and I want to take it in and relax and write and recharge. I could use a day of rest, a full day where we aren't hiking up something."

"I guess I can message my Scotland group and see if I can set up a hike with someone else then. I'm not getting anything out of this trip that I came here for."

"That's a great idea." Savoring the idea of eight glorious hours alone with my keyboard. It sounded heavenly. I felt a little guilty for holding her back, but then pushed it away.

She drove quietly up the hilly stretches of the Scottish Highlands, stopping here and there for sheep to cross the road, pulling over in the pull-outs to let a car pass, and rumbling over the metal livestock barriers. I was so grateful I never had to drive. I was terrified at the prospect of it.

She pulled the car into a nondescript gravel parking lot.

"We're here. Kilt Rock. You'll want to bring your camera."

It was windy and cold, and as I got closer, the sounds of water rushing filled my ears as the misty air got colder and colder. I waited for the best photographic angle to open up and then stepped up and onto the railing.

Furious water cascading down a massive rocky cliff filled my vision. It was beautiful, and the raw power of that rushing water was impressive. The waterfall dropped one hundred and fifty feet, and then the water washed out into the sea. Foamy white surf contrasted with the nearly black rocks and the deep teal blue water. It was beautiful, but an attraction that only took a few minutes maximum to enjoy. We jumped back into the car and winded through more of the stunning Scottish countryside, heading toward our next Airbnb.

THIRTY-FOUR

The next morning, we were back in the car, heading toward Eileen Doan Castle. Erika commented, "I love who I am, Ninya. I truly love myself." I was learning that the people who say that usually really don't, and it was proving true with her.

The night before, she asked for my help to edit the photos of her I took for her website at Finnich Glen.

"My stomach is too big." She analyzed her shape and compared photos. I pulled out my Facetune app and made some adjustments to her favorite one. It was easier than opening a discussion with her about the morality of a personal trainer digitally modifying her photos to look more successful. Photoshop and magazine covers have nearly ruined us all. We have become a heavily filtered people, myself included.

"I'd love to get lip injections, and maybe a leg tuck, and eventually eyelid surgery." She pulled back her eyelids a bit to show me the difference.

"You look great. I mean, come on, you're nearly fifty," I

said, and I meant it. "I mean, if I had unlimited income, I'd most likely have a boob job and some Botox, but at some point, we all have to get to a place where we feel happy in our own skin."

"I am, Ninya. I love myself."

"How can you say that if you want to change so much?"

"I do. I love myself. I know who I am, and I am proud of what I have overcome to become her."

She shrugged off the rest, and I gave up.

A few minutes later, she pulled into a cafe parking lot that had the best view of Eileen Doan Castle. It was an island set out in the sea, with a long bridge leading out to it. The Saltire was waving in the wind. The Scots are a proud people, and their flag was proudly flown throughout the country. I angled for more photos, finding the perfect yellow foreground hedge flowers to frame the castle and the stone bridge. With the mountains in the background, it was a stunning sight. Scotland is covered in castles. Some are ruins, beautiful in their broken way, and some are maintained and used to entertain tourists. The history is so deep and rich, and I was enjoying reading the *Outlander* series while I was there. It made the land come alive when you walked in the same towns that the characters did. It made the whole experience more real. Being there while reading about it gave a romanticized storybook quality to the trip that I savored.

That night, as we wound down to go to sleep, we were both reading. She read a steamy scene aloud from the novel she was reading.

Reading glasses perched on her adorable nose, she said breathily, "'Please... don't.' His answer rang with finality." She paused for dramatic, sexy effect. "Taking control of his betrothed seems natural. Why should she fear it? Women seemed much happier when they were married with children. And being a wife and a mother were the holy duties assigned to females…" She broke character and looked at me, shaking her head, "Motherfucker," she protested, annoyed at the archaic, stereotypical, anti-feministic view.

And I laughed and laughed and laughed. She could be really funny.

THIRTY-FIVE

The next day, we got in the car and drove what seemed like forever, but in reality, it was only five hours. All the stop and go driving was making me nauseous. Up and down, fast and slow, she was shifting like she was a finalist at the Indy 500, and my stomach didn't like it.

At breakfast, she opened her phone and decided we would strike out to find Ploddo Falls, and she navigated us to it step-by-step. I was amazed at her ability to find these obscure places. I knew that, on my own, I would have been driving in circles.

We *did* drive in a few circles that led us down narrow roads with interesting farms and ditches lined with tulips. The most beautiful white blonde Shetland ponies were at the fence line at one of these farms, and we had to stop and take a photo. They walked right up to her, and she loved on them. I witnessed first-hand her deep love for horses, something I never understood but had heard about. I watched her murmur gently to them with soft words and clicks, and then she rubbed her palms down their gorgeous blonde manes. I could feel her sweet energy with them, and it was such a contrast from the other parts of her. She hated to leave them, and I loved being out of the car and away from the nausea, but we continued on.

Wham! She hit a pothole, and we winced, going farther and farther back into what seemed like nowhere, deeper and deeper on one lane roads. The branches were hitting the car, sometimes hard and scraping. It wasn't her fault. I mean, the roads were narrow, and the foliage could be really dense.

WHAM. Another pothole. More wincing.

"These roads are fucked," she declared.

Finally, the car park opened up, she parked, and I gathered my pack and my rain coat. You can nearly count on some sort of precipitation daily in Scotland in May. We walked down a pathway and then up a set of stairs to an observation deck to see Ploddo Falls in all its glory. The water spilled down, hitting the nearly black rocks below. Leaves floated and bobbed along with moss and twigs. The boulders were beautiful. Erika went on ahead like she was used to doing, and I didn't feel like I needed to rush to keep up. I was lost in my own thoughts and the quiet peace of nature.

I wanted to go forest bathing, and this was exactly what my heart needed.

It's too cold to go barefoot here.

I was looking for places to put my feet on the earth like Noah suggested. I was searching for places to reconnect to the earth and reset my hormones. I lost Erika for a bit and just enjoyed the forest, the rocky paths filled with scattered pine needles, and the hilly terrain that was filled with trees covered in moss and lichen from constant dampness. The path was steep and slippery in places, and I enjoyed pushing myself to find the right places to step. I felt a sense of accomplishment, navigating the slick dirt pathways and remaining upright.

Hearing voices ahead, I saw that, across the pond, Erika was chatting with a man who was taking a break on a boulder. The only way over there was to slowly pick your way across the wet stones using a long stick for balance.

Knowing my own limitations, I decided to stay put and not make the journey across. The headache and nausea were gone. Being out of the car was restorative. The air was cool and fresh, and I was grateful for all the layers I wore that kept my feet dry and my body warm.

Suddenly, the need to pee was urgent.

Public bathrooms, for the most part, are unicorns in Scotland. They are nearly nonexistent. Public bathrooms at nature parks are even more scarce. I walked on, searching for a private place to pee, the need to go becoming more urgent with each passing step.

Finally, I found a dead tree that was surrounded by foliage and grasses. If I was quick about it, I could take care of business and be on my way without incident.

I looked around one more time and then took off my pack and squatted into a wall-sit on the dead tree. For a solid minute, I struggled to relax enough to go, constantly on the lookout for people, legs shaking with effort. But finally, blissfully, relief came, and I peed forever.

Thank God. It was a huge accomplishment for my shy bladder.

Completely empty at last, I was able to get back on the trail and walk down a path. I didn't know where Erika was, and I didn't really care at this point. I was just so in love with the forest I was in, the muted light making the colors richer and deeper—oranges from the stones, lime greens from the moss, white from the birch bark. It had started to rain gently, which only made things even more beautiful. I stopped at a magnificent spider web that spanned two feet across, the water droplets kissing the silken threads. It was just so beautiful. The craftsmanship from that insect was truly remarkable.

Then the path opened up with both sides flanked by the largest Douglas firs I had ever seen. Hundreds of years old. Like sentinels standing watch on either side of the path, they practically touched the sky, and I have never felt so small in my entire life. It was spiritual to be in the presence of a living thing that had lived six lifetimes longer than I. The sense of awe and wonder was transcendent. We don't get to experience it as much in life as adults. It filled every corner of my being, pushing away the painful, ugly scars until all I felt in that forest was pure contentment. I saw squirrels and rabbits but not many people, less than ten total the entire time we were there. It was wonderful.

Erika eventually caught up with me. "We should head back," she pointed out.

The rain was falling harder now. Disappointed to leave, but feeling the rain more persistently, we turned and started walking uphill toward the car. She picked her way across the stones and the uphill path easily and quickly. I lingered, knowing that this was an enchanted place and not wanting to break the spell too quickly. I slowly walked in the rain back the way we came, enjoying the massive waterfall one more time, then walking up on the path further to see another wall of waterfalls cascading down the cliff. Such stunning natural beauty. America is a Botox and silicon-filled bimbo compared to the natural curvaceous Marilyn Monroe beauty of Scotland.

THIRTY-SIX

We arrived at our hotel on Loch Ness. I booked it for two days and told Erika to go on a hike without me, that I needed a chill day. So, she met up with another hiker, and I have no idea where they went or what they did, but I didn't care.

The night we got there, the hotel was at maximum capacity, the walls were paper-thin, and a tired baby cried loudly in the room next to us.

"I hope you aren't going to be making noise like this all night!" Erika asserted loudly and rudely. There was no way the people next to us didn't understand her sentiment.

Please, let them not speak English.

She could be demanding and obnoxious. One of my least favorite traits was walking into a pub with her, where she would resoundingly voice her support for President Trump.

Bursting through the door, she would nearly shout, "I love my President! President Trump is the best thing to happen to our country!"

This opinion was always met with astonished confusion,

and I always cringed and slinked away to a dark corner of the pub, pretending not to be with her.

"You can veg here all day today, but you are coming to Hootenanny's with me tonight," she demanded. "Last time we were here, we had so much fun. The music…" She closed her eyes, smiling, fondly remembering her last trip there. "We ended up dancing with the locals all night and then going to an after-hours bar. It was so much fun."

Although the idea of an after-hours bar sounded like a death sentence to an introvert like me, I was feeling a little guilty and wanted to be agreeable. After all, she was giving me a full day to relax at the hotel, blissfully alone, so I wanted to compromise and do something she wanted to do.

She actually made a reservation for us at Hootenanny's that night. Stunned me. Up to that point, I thought she was incapable of doing that. Turns out, she could make reservations, but only if they didn't require a financial commitment.

She left early to meet up with her hiking buddy, and I called my boyfriend back home. The nearly eight-hour time difference was making the calls harder to place.

"Hey, babe!" he answered, and I melted. "How's Scotland?"

"It's so beautiful here. I hope I can bring you back someday."

I told him about my trip to Ploddo Falls.

"That sounds incredible!" he said.

"I just fixed the shower head with a spoon," I told him, proud of myself. "We're in the cheapest Airbnbs, and they are always a crapshoot. Some of them, I am pretty sure, had cockroaches or rats."

"No, thank you."

"I am not a fan of this way of traveling. I like to have a plan. Going to be booking our flights today."

"You're doing the smart thing," he confirmed.

"We are such different people. She doesn't understand me, but I don't need her to."

"That's right, babe. You don't. Sounds like your encounters with her should be a book."

"She's a character for sure. We'll see."

We talked a bit more, and I talked to my daughter, and then I hung up, missing home again.

I stretched my tired legs and then grabbed my makeshift laptop and went to the bright and sunny restaurant. It was all windows and on the third floor, with sweeping views that overlooked Loch Ness. Magnificent mountains and water as far as your eye could see, it was beautiful. I took a photo of my laptop on the table with the window view.

This is my dream. This is what I want to do for the rest of my life. Go on adventures with my laptop and write anywhere and everywhere.

I have a weakness for scallops, and I was excited to splurge on a great meal with fresh scallops without Erika dragging me to yet another fish and chips cheap dining experience.

The waitress handed me the menu at the bar, and I was sad to see that scallops were not on the lunch menu. Devastated, I did something totally out of character for a chronic settler like me. I asked, "I was hoping to have scallops for lunch, but I don't see them on the menu. Does that mean it's not available?"

"Not on the lunch menu, but let me talk to the chef," the sweet waitress replied, and then she walked to the kitchen to confer with the chef while I waited.

If you don't ask for what you want, you'll never get it.

Five minutes later, she returned.

"Looks like today is your lucky day. He never does this but said he is bored back there and is going to do it for you."

I clapped my hands together. "Thank you so much!" I

ordered some Cullen skink to start and waited for the scallops to arrive.

Sitting by the window with the sun flooding in was decadent. Light has always been so important to me. Something I have always craved since I learned to study it in photography school. I opened my journal and started writing. An obsessive list maker, I cranked this out:

What am I learning here?

> *To advocate for myself and for what I need.*

> *To speak up for myself.*

> *To accept myself like the introvert I am and to not see that as a flaw.*

> *I am lucky to be here having this experience at all. My mom did not get this chance, and Lesley didn't get this chance.*

> *Nature is restorative. Being out in the forest has been incredibly healing, and I need to make more time for that.*

> *Things at home will be okay without my constant micromanagement.*

> *I am good enough the way I am, without Ryan's approval or him wanting to share his life with me.*

> *Everyone is broken and scarred in their own ways. We all carry the pain of our pasts in our bodies, and it is our job to find it and release it.*

> *There is enough for me. In every way. Always enough.*

> *I can adapt to almost any situation and to almost any person.*

> *There is power in being quiet and not jumping to conclusions all the time.*

> *Being reactionary is exhausting and a waste of time and effort.*

The scallops arrived, and they were legendary. Seared to perfection in creamy, salty butter, a bacon sauce spooned on top, scattered with gorgeous microgreens on a long rectangular white plate. I savored the hell out of them, eating them slowly, tasting the sea and the salty bacon contrasting in the most exquisite way. I looked at the menu again and saw Sticky Toffee Pudding.

What the hell. When in the UK...

I mean, you have to try the local delicacies when you travel, right? If not, you miss out on half of the experience.

I wrote and wrote—some journaling, some on projects I was working on—and it was the absolute perfect day. I mean, seared scallops, sticky toffee pudding, and a feast of words. What more could an aspiring writer ask for? Around four, I tipped the waiter and the chef well and went back to the room. I wanted to book the airplane tickets we needed to get from Scotland to Ireland since we were flying home from Dublin. Not having airplane tickets a mere eight days before we needed them was nearly giving me heart palpitations at night.

I asked Erika about it, and she chastised, "Relax, Ninya. Let's wait. I don't even know what I'm doing tomorrow."

This "not booking anything trip" was a little crazy. I wanted to plan the rest of it, the next three days of hikes we wanted to take, and where we were going to stay.

She was getting frustrated with my need to know where we were staying and how we were getting to Dublin.

"I just like to have a general idea and know what is coming," I explained, trying to make my feelings known in a gentle way. In reality, I was nearly puking inside from the anxiety of the unknown. Being in a foreign country with no lodging was very unsettling to a type A person like me.

"We'll play it by ear. You can't plan everything." She was getting exasperated with my constant need to know where we were staying and how we were getting there. "Just let me focus on today."

So, I let her, but that night before she got back from her day of hiking, I booked the airline tickets anyway. Then I started to get ready for our trip to Hootenanny's that night, not knowing the craziest part of the trip was getting ready to unfold.

THIRTY-SEVEN

Hair curled up and dressed in the only non-yoga pants I put in my suitcase, we headed to Hootenanny's. The drive was nearly thirty minutes of the curviest roads without any shoulder, next to the large body of water that is Loch Ness. In the city of Inverness, finding parking is a bitch. The kind of bitch that talks in circles and leaves you frustrated.

Erika dropped me at the door, and I went in to find our table so we wouldn't lose our reservation. That turned out to be a good thing because it was the only table left. I took the seat that faced the door so I could see Erika when she walked in, and it also happened to face the table where the band was setting up. I use the term *band* loosely because it was literally two guys with fiddles and banjos and other stringed instruments.

After about ten minutes, Erika finally came in. When she saw the seat that was left for her, she ranted, "This sucks. I'm not going to be able to see anything at all."

It is music. You don't need to see it.

She stood there, pouting and looking at the table, refusing to sit, so I asked, "Do you want to switch seats?" I thought she would refuse. After all, she was here two years ago and already got to experience this.

"Yes," she admitted, shocking me, and I tried not to roll my eyes as I picked up my jacket and drink to switch seats with her.

Wow. Selfish much?

Then she proceeded to use the best seat at our table to look down at her phone for the next hour. Obviously, she was sexting her husband back home because she was giggling and saying naughty things under her breath, and I was more than a little frustrated.

The folksy Celtic music was beautiful, and I turned my chair completely around to face the men playing.

At some point, Erika went to the bar and stood. In a pub, this was always her chosen spot. There, she always found a new influx of people and would strike up conversations with them. Two younger men came in and sat down in front of me. They apologized profusely for sitting in front of me, blocking my view, and I smiled and waved the comment off, saying, "No problem," and continued to listen to the music. The band took a break, and we struck up a conversation. They were Canadian brothers having a holiday in Scotland and were wild camping, which is just camping in the forest, not at a commercial campground. They would hike all day and then set up their tents wherever they got the urge. Both of them were funny and hitting the whiskey pretty hard, and I was finally enjoying myself when Erika appeared standing at my side and inserted herself into the conversation.

Hearing that they were Canadian, she threw in an ill-timed, "Eh," and then all hell broke loose.

One of the brothers didn't pull any punches and said to her directly, "That was rude and obnoxious."

She was instantly incensed, saying, "Are you kidding me?

I have tons of Canadian friends, and we make fun of their accents all the time."

He stood up his entire six feet and got closer to her, and shot back, "No. I am not kidding."

More choruses of, "You've got to be kidding me," and "No, I am not," continued. They were, in fact, not kidding her, but she couldn't seem to grasp it.

I was riveted, mostly because I got the sense that this never happened to Erika in real life. There was a steam roller quality to her that most people were afraid or unwilling to call her out on, but not this guy. At that moment, he kind of became my hero.

"You're familiar with Trump?" he asked.

"I love him," she confessed smugly.

"Then you know all about the wall." He moved his arm up in front of her, clearly defining where his space was and where her side began. "Here's the wall. Stay on your side."

I was dying for popcorn at this point, but alas, there was none.

"How old are you?" she shot back as if that was relevant.

"Thirty-three," he answered.

"Figures, fucking snowflake," she shouted.

At that point, he was done with her. When they walked to the bar for another drink, she stormed off, leaving me at the table alone.

The music cued up again, and the men returned, sipping their whiskey. I could hear them say to each other, "I am not going to let an obnoxious American treat me like that. Let's get out of here." Then they left. I could see Erika out of the corner of my eye at the bar, surrounded by a group of older men. She waved at me, trying to get me to come over, but I was not in the mood after that exchange so I stayed away. She was in her element, surrounded by men, flexing, laughing, and carrying on. I just sat and listened to the music.

A few hours later, it was nearly midnight, and the pub was emptying out, so I gathered my things. Hoping to convince Erika to leave, I went to the bar where she was speaking with two English chaps. And they were authentic English chaps, one wearing the prerequisite newsboy hat. Childhood friends, they were on a golf holiday with a big group who had left them at Hootenanny's in favor of the strip club down the street.

One was a judge, and the other was a lumber salesman, both very successful men, both named Duncan. Erika introduced them to me, and the royal baby had just been born, so I led with that.

The judge smiled and said, "Everyone is in love with Archie. Just over the moon." The lumber magnate bought us a round of drinks, more pear cider was consumed, and we chatted about random things.

"You came to Scotland with someone you *never* met before?"

"Yes."

They were very shocked.

"Are you sharing a bed?"

"Most of the time, we are to save money," I answered. Their eyes got big.

They shared stories of their college days, sharing rooms, and how sometimes when they travel, they still share rooms to have the company. We laughed about how awkward it is when you accidentally touch the person lying in bed next to you.

"What do you do?" they asked.

"I am a photographer and blogger." I got out my phone and showed them a few photos.

"Can you take our picture so we can be on your blog?" they inquired.

"Well, I don't know why I wouldn't." I winked and

laughed and took them to the doorway for better light, which was still terrible that late at night in a pub, and took their photo.

It was pretty loud in there, and the lumber magnate said, "You need to put yourself out there more. You need to let people see you. My partner got sick last year, and it makes you figure out what's really important in life."

Hmm. Strangers are sometimes messengers from God. Maybe he's right.

"My mom died a few years ago, and I agree with you. Puts things in perspective really quickly," I answered.

Finally, I finished my drink and set it on the bar, and since Erika's glass was nearly empty, I was hoping she'd get the hint so we could call it a night.

She finished her glass and put it on the bar, and the bell rang for last call.

"One more round," the lumber magnate declared and threw down more pounds. I refused another drink, not wanting to feel sick the next day, but everyone else put an order in and had to drink them quickly since it was closing time. The barkeep pushed us to the door. The cool air hit us, and that's when I saw Erika first stumble while walking a little bit. Then she giggled. I watched her carefully, getting very concerned about her ability to drive the nearly thirty minutes back to our hotel.

Oh shit. Is she drunk?

"You know what we should do?" she asked. "Go to the strip club and drag your friends out by their ears."

Lumber magnate was on board with this idea, and he and the judge laughed hysterically at the embarrassment potential and decided it was a great plan. They were literally nearly peeing themselves with excitement at their mate's future humiliation.

As I watched Erika walk, I was starting to wonder if she *could* drive.

"Maybe you should call an Uber," the judge advised. "It's not worth the risk to drive when you're pissed."

Pissed was slang for drunk.

"I'm fine," she dismissed, walking a little straighter. I couldn't really tell if she was or not.

The bouncer at the door looked at our rag tag group of old fuckers and let us in anyway. Erika walked into the strip club ahead of us boldly, and the Englishmen's friends were nowhere to be found. She did, however, walk up to a dancer, who had to have been about twenty-two, and slapped her bottom before shaking her own a little bit. Then over her shoulder, she said, "I have a better ass than most of the strippers in here."

It couldn't possibly be true. I mean, half a century of gravity changes a woman, but I nodded and continued to monitor her for signs of drunkenness.

We all walked outside, them laughing, me lost in anxiety. The English gents pulled out their phones, trying to find an Uber or a Lyft.

"Helloooo, Inverness!" she shouted, her words echoing off buildings and the cobblestone streets.

We walked to the car.

"Are you sure you can drive?" I asked.

"Yeah, I'm totally fine."

"Are you *sure*?" I asked again, the worry creeping in my voice, scanning my surroundings for a coffee shop that was open, but there were none.

"Yes," she said. "I am okay to drive." I was a little relieved since there was still a thirty-minute car ride we needed to take to get back to our hotel. I ushered her back to our car while the English chaps followed us. I was motivated to get her in the car and back to our hotel, the sooner the better.

At the car, she asked, "Do you guys need a ride?" and my heart dropped.

Why? Just why? These are men of means. They can find and pay for a ride back to their hotel on their own.

"Yes, that would be brilliant," they said.

Fuck. Fuck. Fuck.

We all jumped into the car. The lumber magnate sat next to Erika, and the judge was in the backseat next to me.

"Okay. Okay. I need to focus," she said. She adjusted the rearview mirror and took a deep breath.

She put the car in drive, and the lumber magnate made jokes and started talking loudly.

"Shut the fuck up!" She screamed in his face, and we were stunned. The judge and I exchanged looks in the back of the car. Lumber magnate laughed, thinking it was a joke and then continued, even louder.

She was driving erratically, all over the place, and I asked the judge, "I've got a piece of paper here. Do you want to write an explanation on it in case we all die tonight so you don't cause a scandal in your country?"

He laughed, and we hung on to the seats in front of us for dear life. Careening down the streets of Inverness, shifting hard, we were fingertips away from the parked cars on the narrow streets. My anxiety was at a near record high.

Lumber magnate started telling jokes again and laughing at them in the front seat.

"SHUT THE FUCK UP!" She screamed over and over. He was confused, and we sat in awkward silence for the rest of the trip, until finally, their hotel appeared. I had never been happier to see a swanky boutique hotel entrance in my life. She parked the car too close to the others in a space that wasn't even a parking space and announced, "I have to piss."

Like a *lady.*

And then she followed them into their hotel, while I sat in

the car, weighing my options. I wasn't sure what to do next when I heard a little knock on the window. It was the judge. I rolled down the window and smiled weakly.

He crouched down to my eye level and asked, "Are you okay?"

"Yes." My eyes were huge. I shook my head, unable to believe the bizarre reality that had been unfolding.

"A few words come to mind, and one of them is psycho," he said.

We both laughed.

"You are correct, sir." I smiled and nodded.

"How far do you need to drive to get to your hotel?" he asked.

"Twenty minutes."

"I am afraid for you."

"That makes two of us," I admitted.

We said our goodbyes, and Erika finally stumbled back to the car. It took nearly fifteen minutes of maneuvering to back the car out of that illegal parking place.

She concentrated on following the GPS directions back to our hotel.

"Watch it," I pleaded, deeply concerned with every swerve of the car, scanning the roads for obstacles and police cars.

"You're too close to the parked cars," I warned. I closed my eyes and braced myself for impact, praying we'd make it home in one piece while wondering what automobile accident protocol with a rental car was in a foreign country. I was hyper-vigilant and micromanaging her driving. "Stay in your lane. You almost hit that car."

"I know. I know. I see it," she insisted impatiently. "You need to stop. You're making me nervous."

"Just trying to help," I replied, but I could see it had the opposite effect, so I decided to stay quiet. A few minutes later, we entered a roundabout. She swerved again to miss a rabbit in the roundabout, then hit the gas hard. I gasped when I saw the blue and white lights flash.

We were being pulled over.

In a foreign country.

In a rental car.

On my credit card.

And the driver is probably drunk.

My heart raced, and I instantly wanted to throw up.

Am I going to jail?

Is she going to jail?

Will the car be impounded?

Holy Fuck. Holy Fuck. Holy Fuck.

"Are we going to be okay?" she asked and then took a long sip of water and popped a mint in her mouth. Looking in the rearview mirror, she smoothed her hair.

"We have to be," I answered woodenly. I was in shock.

The officer came to her side of the car, and she rolled down the window.

We are fucked.

She gets out of this car, someone is going to jail.

There is no way she would pass a field sobriety test.

"De ya know why we stopped ye?" he asked, puffing on a vape.

I answered for her, leaning forward to make eye contact with the officer. "She's an insane animal lover and saw a bunny in the roundabout. I told her just to hit it, but she was afraid she'd kill it."

"And when ye came out of the roundabout, you were ten ov'r the limit."

"Oh, we were? I'm so sorry. I didn't know what the speed limit was, Officer," She answered sweetly to the young Scot.

"Are ye on holiday?"

"Yes, sir," I said and laughed nervously. "We're Americans."

"I could tell from ye accents." He smiled and looked us both up and down, quietly considering his next move.

After the longest pause in history, he said, "Well, then pay more attention and get on yer way."

And then he let us go. LET US GO!

He walked back to his squad car, got in, and drove away. We were both shaking, the relief flooding in.

"I can't believe it," I said. "You were so lucky."

"I know." She laughed in relief.

Then she started driving us back to the hotel, the traffic stop sobering her up quickly. I sat next to her, silent. The rage built, terrified that every turn we took on the road would land us at the bottom of Loch Ness. We got to the hotel and parked the car. Relieved that we'd finally arrived in one piece, I went inside, and I grabbed the phone to call Ryan while she got ready for bed. Shaking with anger now that the fear had dissipated, I walked to the hallway and rode the elevator down two stories, then ranted to Ryan for an hour. Rage whispering at three a.m. because of the thin walls about the events of the night while he tried to calm me down. After it all came out, I was exhausted and ready for bed. The idea of getting into a shared bed with someone I wanted to kill was hard to swallow, but the exhaustion won, and I did it anyway. The only sound was Erika passed out, snoring in the bed next to me.

THIRTY-EIGHT

I t was a short night. Three hours later, morning came, and we packed up silently before moving to the next town on our trip. The passive aggressive vibe was thick, and we avoided each other. I have never been more grateful for the existence of headphones in my entire life.

You are stuck. You are here. Make the most of this trip.

Why are you here with this woman right now?

What cosmic flip of the universe conspired to make this happen?

God has a huge fucking sense of humor, or I am in hell, the fourth ring of hell, some kind of foreign traveler with a crazy companion hell.

She drove silently toward Cairngorms National Park. I was done interacting with her and needed a break, so I listened to podcasts all the way, trying to reset my brain and change my mindset, but the frustration and anger were lodged there.

YOU ARE IN SCOTLAND. Do not let her ruin this for you.

She parked the car and met her hiking buddy in Aviemore. I didn't think to ask her for the car keys so I could have access to all my things while she was gone for the day hiking. My plan was to walk a bit, sit a bit, write a bit, and decompress from the events of the prior evening.

With only my raincoat and the backpack, I wandered around and found a pretty trail near the nicest hostel I have ever seen. Sitting on a cold rock, I pulled out the phone and called Ryan. He picked up on the first ring. His voice broke my heart, missing home so fiercely at that moment, it made me tear up.

"She's crazy," I exclaimed. "We haven't talked at all. She's hiking right now, and I am stuck here without my things because, like an idiot, I forgot to ask her for the car keys. We have no place to stay tonight, and she won't even tell me what town we'll be in so I can book an Airbnb."

"Leave her. Get on a train and leave her there. You went there to heal yourself."

"But the car, babe, it's on my credit card."

"Return the car ASAP and go your separate ways. You can do that. I will send you whatever you need. You can figure it out. You don't need her."

I was starting to think he had a point.

"Noah was right," Ryan said.

"I know." I sighed, exasperated from the events of the night before. "Don't worry, I came here to heal myself, and I will not let her ruin this for me."

"You better not. This is another test. A really expensive one, but still it is in your hands. You control your destiny."

"God, I miss you so much."

"I miss you, too, babe. Return the car, go your separate ways, and enjoy the rest of the trip as much as you can."

I was afraid still, not sure I could do it alone.

"I'll think about it. I love you and miss you."

"Love you, too."

Not sure what it is about being thousands of miles away,

but it makes your heart ache. Words are all you have to cling to, not the touches or the physical embraces, just the words, and they mean so much.

We hung up, and I put my pack back on and continued up the trail. I had no idea where I was going but followed a random trail that led me to this incredibly beautiful bird sanctuary. Hilly terrain covered in trees with winding walkways. The sun peeked in and out of clouds in a forest. I followed the trail. My frustration with Erika and the events of the prior evening clouded and consumed my thoughts.

Stop it. Stop wallowing in this pile of ick.

I pushed them away, continuing to walk past a small pond filled with ducks. I walked deeper into the woods, and the birds and my feet crunching on the grass and rocks were the only sound.

When you are in Scotland, reflect in your mom's shoes. When she was not talking to you for four years, what was she feeling?

Such a loaded question. I felt like an orphan at the time, but both my parents were still living. Mom had cut off all contact when I was a young mother with a new baby on the way, and I never understood why. My dad had started a new family and had kids the *same* age as mine, and he was focused on his new wife and new family, leaving the old one behind. I needed them both, and they had deserted me. My parents had gotten divorced when I was an adult, and my mom assumed I had taken Dad's side, and so she just disappeared. She loved babies and was excited to be a grandma, but something happened to her after the divorce. She became a different person, forcing us to choose between her and Dad.

There was no contact for four years, and then a phone call out of the blue one day. "Ninya, this is Mom. I need to talk to you. It's important."

This was the call I had been waiting for, and I called her back immediately. We set a time to see each other at her apartment, and I went there with my sister, not knowing what to expect but filled with hope that something might change, that she might be part of my life again. I missed her so much, and I wanted that relationship back. When I arrived, I saw she was the same person. Living simply in an apartment with my brother in a small town.

We sat down at her old worn out linoleum table. She was quiet, searching for the right words, then she said, "I have some news. I went to the doctor, and it is not good. I have cancer, and I have decided not to have chemotherapy."

I sat in shock with my sister. We were silent. Stunned. This is not what I expected at all.

"Pancreatic. It's very difficult to keep any kind of food down."

That's one of the worst types to get. Survival rate is nearly zero. Patrick Swayze just died from that. Mom's had the biggest crush on him since Dirty Dancing.

Random associations had become my brain's coping mechanism whenever met with painful realities.

"I wanted to tell you myself and let you know what my last wishes are so there's no confusion. I don't want you to have to worry about anything or to have to take care of me. When it is time, I will go into hospice. I have already met with them, and it is all set up. I don't want a funeral, or for anyone to look at my body. I don't want to burden you financially, so when the time comes, you can call the state. They have a special fund for the final expenses for people that can't afford a funeral. Everything has already been taken care of."

I heard the words like she was talking about a stranger, like they were the plot to a book she was reading.

Tears rolled down my face. *Wait. No. This can't be true. I want a do-over. I thought we were gonna get a do-over. Why is she talking about final arrangements and worrying about worrying us?*

I want my mom back. I thought I was going to get my mom back today.

"I wish things had been different. I wasted so much time, and I regret that." She was somber and serious, her eyes watery, but her voice strong and resolute.

NO! NO! NO! This can't be happening.

But it was.

The panic of her time clock counting down started. The knowledge that there was a finite amount of time available made everything more important. She seemed like she always was that day, maybe a little more serious and introspective, but she didn't *look* sick. I wanted her to meet my daughter, and I wanted us to have a photoshoot before she started feeling too bad to do it. Being a photographer, I knew how important a last family portrait was when your mother had cancer. So, we left her apartment with the words, "Let us know when you are up for it, and we will bring the kids over to see you." She'd never met my daughter, and suddenly, it seemed *so* important to me for them to know each other.

She was living in the apartment alone with my brother, and I told him, "Call me if you need help with Mom." But he never did. I waited for her to tell me she was ready to see the kids, but with the four-year spilt, there was an awkwardness that I struggled to overcome. I didn't want to force them on her, but I shouldn't have waited.

A few weeks later, my brother called, panicked.

"She's sick, Neen. So sick."

"Why didn't you call me?"

"She didn't want to burden you. I called hospice. I didn't know what else to do." He sobbed into the phone.

I got in the car immediately and drove the thirty minutes to her hospice. She was full of drugs making her more comfortable. She slept a lot, but sometimes the pain would wake her up or I would hear her cry out. The physical difference was remarkable. She was thin, her cheeks hollow. Pancreatic cancer makes it impossible to eat, and so in just a few weeks, she was a shell of the woman we met at the apartment. The physical manifestation of cancer is devastating, consuming and eating away at a person until there is nothing left. It is brutal to watch someone you love being ravaged by its effects.

I sat vigil for days, not wanting to leave her side, trying to make up for the lost time so she wouldn't transition to the next place alone. And the emotion I felt most was regret. Why had we both been so stupid? Why didn't I pick up the phone and say, "Mom, this is dumb. I don't know what this is about or how we got here, but it's not important. Let's just start over."

I sat at her bedside for nearly a week, unable to leave for fear of missing even one moment of lucidity. Three days before she died, she had one clear moment. She looked right into my eyes and said, "Don't believe what other people have told you about me. I always loved you." That was the last thing she ever said to me, and I was so grateful for that last brief moment of clarity.

I took a picture of my brother holding her hand. We all got a chance to say our goodbyes, and then a few days later, when my sister made it from Chicago, she passed away in her sleep. Somehow, she knew that we were all finally gathered together in one place. We told her it was okay to go, and she passed quietly. I placed a purple orchid in her hair, and then they took her away to be cremated. It happened so fast and left such a void in my heart. I was devastated. When you lose your mom, it feels like you have lost your lifeline. You are like a boat floating out to sea with no anchor. You feel lost.

What was she feeling?
She felt left out and alone. I felt like an orphan.

How was Liam feeling?

Like an orphan. Although the circumstances were different, when we put him in a residential treatment program, he had to feel like he was alone, like he didn't have parents. We made the decision to do it based on what was happening and what the experts told us needed to be done to fix it, but it created such division. He felt alone.

I needed you, Mom. I just wanted my mom. I wish you were around to help me when things went off the rails with Liam. I didn't know what to do.

I walked, tears blurring my vision as I climbed up rocky paths with wildflowers, the sun peaking in and out of the clouds. A gentle rain that is quintessential Scotland would fall on my face from time to time, washing the tears away, then it would all dry again as the sun came out.

I forgive you. I forgive you for not knowing how to fix it. I forgive you for not knowing better and doing the best you could do for us. I know your childhood was difficult, and I know that you ended up with my dad because you wanted to be rescued from your life and thought he would be your ticket out of poverty and pain at seventeen. I know you did your best. I am just so sad that your best wasn't able to see past the divorce and our want to have both of our parents in our lives. That it wasn't an either-or situation. We needed you both.

I forgive you. I forgive you. I forgive you.

I chanted over and over, fresh tears combining with rain drops again, washing away the years of pain and neglect.

My mom's birthday was October 8, and my baby's due date had been October 11.

Hold my baby for me, Mom. Take care of this one that I never got to hold.

There was the smallest amount of comfort I got from visualizing my mom in heaven, rocking my unborn baby. She was always so great with babies. She had such a gentle touch and would swaddle them up and gently place them in the crook of her neck, then bobbing up and down would sing little made up songs to calm them down. I prayed that, somehow, my unborn baby ended up in her arms, finding comfort and love there.

I had recovered physically from the termination, but emotionally, it was still heavy and still weighed on me. I will carry the burden of that decision forever. The moments of quiet were the hardest, the litany of thoughts and regrets filled my quiet spaces. Regret changes who you are and becomes a part of the fabric of your being. It leeches on and has everlasting life. There will never be a time when I won't wish things had been different. That it had never happened. But it did, and in order to survive, I had to set down the guilt. The weight of it was so massive and self-destructive it would consume my life if I let it. I had to forgive myself and beg for forgiveness from God. On judgment day, I will have a lot of explaining to do, but my God is a father. A father *loves* first and foremost. He is not this fire and brimstone figure that enjoys condemning a person to hell. I have asked for forgiveness, and I believe I have been given grace.

I stopped near a stream and took off my shoes, looking to ground myself and reset my hormones like Noah instructed. I pulled out my iPad and wrote about the experience, about what I was learning, about the regrets I had. It was the most miraculous and beautiful place I have ever had the opportunity to write. With my toes on a cool boulder covered in moss, the freshest air I had ever smelled, and the tinkling of water trickling over stones and down the hill, it was so peaceful and centering.

This is what I came here to do. No one was going to take that away from me, and I was proud that I accomplished that monumental task.

I don't need Erika to have my breakthroughs. I can do that on my own.

It started to really rain heavily then, so I packed up everything and walked out of that forest. I was finally at peace with my mom's passing and had fully forgiven her. I left all the negativity and pain there in that forest on that path. I understood Liam much more fully, and I saw the part I played in his fear and how fear and control ruined things with him. I saw the orphan dynamic that Noah talked about. When he first said that it repeated with Liam, I was shocked and didn't understand it. Now, I fully did.

The day I spent at the bird sanctuary in Aviemore was the most healing experience of the trip for me. It was exactly what I came here to do, and I didn't need Erika to accomplish that.

THIRTY-NINE

I walked in a torrential downpour a mile to a pizza place, thanking the Wi-Fi gods for a great connection and edible pizza. Erika was still hiking, and it was nearly four p.m. We still had no place lined up to stay yet. I didn't even consult her; I just found the nearest Airbnb to us and booked it.

An hour later, I got the message that Erika was back, so I met her at the car.

"It was incredible. We got almost to the summit, and it was so cold. Snowing!"

She was happy and excited, the endorphins still coursing through her body.

"I booked an Airbnb. It's only twenty minutes from here."

"That's the opposite way. We'll be back-tracking."

"You didn't make any plans, so I did. He has a washing machine, and I'm tired."

"It's out of the way."

"Too bad. It's done," I insisted, leaving no room for argument.

We headed there in silence, the weight of the night before

still heavy between us. Neither of us wanted to say much about it.

We got to the little cottage pretty quickly, and it was the sweetest and homiest place we stayed the entire trip.

"We have two bedrooms available tonight. This one with two twin beds or the double," our host said, a sweet red-headed older Scot. His voice had a gentle, musical quality with a thick Scottish accent.

"This is perfect," I said, quickly scooping up the room with the twin beds. I needed physical space from her, and sharing a bed to save money was getting tiresome.

I walked into the room and immediately wanted to take a shower to warm up. Erika walked back downstairs, talking with our host, and I heard them laughing and jabbering and was glad she wasn't in the room with me. I showered and then started to read and fell asleep quickly and early. I woke with the sun coming through the skylight the next morning. Erika was still asleep, so I got my phone and my ear buds and pulled up a podcast, still lying in bed, waiting for her to wake up. I have always loved Oprah's *Super Soul* series, so I opened up a random episode with Maryanne Williamson.

"Every relationship is an assignment made by the universe to foster the creativity of the universe. It does not mean we will necessarily like each other. It's easy to be enlightened when everyone is being really nice to you and doing exactly what you want them to do, but there is no growth in that. We are assigned to people with whom we have the maximum opportunity for soul growth. Relationships are laboratories of the spirit."

Whoa. The perfect words at the perfect time. Sometimes God gets it right.

Erika was *assigned* to me by the universe? This is giving me the opportunity for *maximum* soul growth? Apparently, God has an incredible sense of humor.

I was feeling the anger about the night at Hootenanny's dissipating, which was good. I wanted to enjoy the rest of our time in Scotland as much as possible, but I knew we would have to have a conversation about it to put it to rest, and so I packed up my bags, finally in the right frame of mind to have it. Maryanne Williamson had opened up my mind to the reason why we were put together on this Scottish pilgrimage. Her words strengthened my resolve and my spirit. They opened my mind to the strengths Erika had as a woman.

"Relationships are laboratories of the spirit."

I was ready to start my greatest work and undertake my greatest experiment, a conversation to clear the air and process what had happened two nights before. It was going to be difficult, but I was going to do it.

WE DROVE QUIETLY for a while toward Pitlochry and were planning to hike at the Hermitage on the way. I was listening to another podcast and trying to get ready for the impending confrontation. We got into town and stopped at a Tesco to get some sandwiches and snacks that we would eat on our hike.

Back in the car, I finally broached the subject. Words were always harder for me to find when speaking than they ever were when writing. Coupled with the tension of speaking my mind for the first time in my life, directly and openly, with a woman who was very opinionated and strong, I struggled to find the right words to say.

"I think we should talk about what happened," I started nervously.

She kept driving so I continued.

"You put me at risk, physically and financially. We could have gone to jail. They could have impounded the car."

"But we didn't," she dismissed.

"That's not the point. You should have been more responsible. You knew we were half an hour from the hotel, so you should have stopped drinking so you could sober up to drive."

"What do you want me to say? That I'm sorry?"

"It would be a start."

"I *am* sorry. But nothing happened."

Reaching a dead end, I tried a different tactic. "We definitely came here for different reasons," I tried to explain. "I came here to rest and replenish and heal myself. You want to go out all the time, and that is not my thing. I mean, I can't afford to drink at the pub every night, and I don't want to ruin our hikes because I feel shitty the next day."

"Our hikes?" She chuckled. "What hikes? You weren't prepared to hike. You're not in good enough shape," she countered, on the attack. "I came here to hike, and I am getting nothing from this trip."

"I told you that before we came. I was depressed. It was a monumental task just to get out of bed most days, and you said it was totally fine, that we would have so much fun anyway."

"I *did* drink too much," She finally admitted. "I guess I am more anxious being around an introvert who is constantly smashing the keyboard. It's making me drink more."

What? You're blaming me?

"And you're so loud when you talk to your kids on the phone."

Seriously?

The heat was rising up in my chest, and I was getting angry. In defense mode, I hit her with a truth bomb.

"You're too much. You demand all the attention when you walk in a room. Don't you see that people are reflecting back to you the energy you give them?"

"What do you mean?"

"The waitress, the Canadians? All the flexing and screaming out Trump's name when we walk into a pub? You are dying for attention. Desperate for it."

"Are you just keeping track of everything?"

She was getting angrier and angrier, and then she abruptly pulled into a parking lot. The town was crawling with people, walking down the adorable sidewalks in Pitlochry.

"Look, Erika, we can do one of two things. We can return the car today and go our separate ways, or we can stay together. If we stay together, I am going to want to do what I came here to do. Walk in the forests, write, have some quiet time. I don't want to go out every night, drinking in the pubs. I came here to heal myself, and I am not going back home without having done that. People sacrificed in order for me to come here. I will not let them down."

She turned to me abruptly. "No one has ever spoken to me the way you speak to me."

Maybe someone should.

"It's the truth, Erika. It keeps coming up, over and over again. Can't you see that?"

"I have never been so insulted. You don't know me!" she shouted heatedly.

"You're right. I don't know you. All I can go on is what you've told me this last week and what I've seen from your actions."

She busied herself, organizing the stuff in the console, looking for something.

"Let's just return the car in Glasgow and go our separate ways. We obviously want different things from this trip. Let's just get rid of the car and say goodbye," I suggested.

She studied me for a second, weighing things in her mind.

"I have to call my husband," she said abruptly.

She left me in the car and walked away. I scrambled to call Ryan on the phone he gave me.

"Pick up. Pick up," I begged quietly, and then hearing his voice was a relief.

"I told her we need to get rid of the car and go our separate ways."

"Sounds like the best plan for both of you."

"She's crazy, babe. I just want to be free. I can figure out the bus and train to see what I want to see for the last four days anyway. I gotta go. Here she comes." I hung up and put the phone in my backpack.

She strode to the car, and I heard her click the trunk button. I waited for her to come to the front, but it was taking an inordinate amount time, so I opened the door to see what the hold-up was. She was organizing her luggage and packing things up, zipping and unzipping compartments feverishly.

"I don't care what you do. I'm leaving." She hoisted her pack to her shoulders.

"What?" I asked, not comprehending at all what she said.

"I'm getting on a train and getting the fuck out of here. No one has ever spoken to me like you have. No one has ever treated me like you have. It's insulting the way you speak to me."

We were two hours from where we needed to be to drop off the car. The panic was hot and fresh.

"You can't do that. We *have* to return this car."

"*I* don't have to do anything." She continued to pack up her things, enraged.

Panic ensued, and I began pleading with her. "I cannot legally drive this car. You know that. You were the one who insisted on being the only driver so we could save fifty pounds."

"Not my problem," she stated coldly as she pulled her

luggage out of the trunk. I was stunned and desperate to get her to change her mind. "You're probably going to blog about this anyway, and I don't even care. I don't want to be around you anymore, either."

"Erika, we *have* to return this car," I insisted, trying to reason with her.

"Figure it out. You knew how to drive a stick, you said. I'm done. Ninya, I am *SO* done."

"That was almost thirty years ago and on the other side of the street. I don't even know where we are. I don't have any navigation device since the only SIM card is on your phone," I pleaded.

I was panicking. The car was on my credit card. She didn't care because it didn't affect her at all. If the car wasn't ever returned, they were coming after me.

"We are both adults. Let's be responsible *women* and return the car and then part ways," I reasoned.

She said nothing, firm in her resolve to leave.

"You can't do this. You can't leave me in a town I don't know with a car I can't drive."

She finally had all her things together. She paused and stared at the trunk, trying to make a final decision.

My brain searched for the right words to say, knowing I had to apologize. It was the only way to get this car returned, but I didn't want to lie, so I said the only thing I could that was true.

"I am sorry. I can be judgmental. It's a trait I hate about myself, but I am working on it."

She stopped for a moment, carefully considering my words.

I went deeper.

"You are a force to be reckoned with. You walk into a room and own it. I never have the balls to do that. We're very different people, but I am grateful for you showing me this country. I know I would have never gotten to see a fraction of what I have gotten to see without you."

She waited. I felt her resolve weakening.

"Let's not do this. This can't be the end. Let's finish the trip and part ways without becoming enemies," I begged. "We're here, so let's hike," I said, hoping that her want to hike would overshadow her desire to leave.

She looked at me. "How do I know that your apology is real, and you aren't just telling me what I want to hear to get what you want?"

While there was certainly an element of that, I was also proud of myself for being honest.

"It's the truth. I can appreciate our differences. We aren't ever going to be best friends, but we shared this experience, and to leave it like this just isn't right."

"Let's hike," she said decisively, those two words ushering in almost as much relief as when the police officer let us go.

Making up her mind, she put her bags back into the trunk and shut it, and we drove to the Hermitage to hike. I was relieved, but more than that, I was proud of myself. I stood up to an Alpha woman, a strong, former military, tough as nails bitch, and I spoke up for myself. I was getting stronger.

FORTY

The Hermitage was home to one of the most beautiful waterfalls I have ever seen. We picked along the path. The air was clearer between us than it had been in the last few days, the tension of the car and the crazy night in Inverness gone. Thankfully, years of trauma have given me a unique skill. I can package whatever crappy feeling or event has happened into a little box and then fling it out and away, where it still lives but is forgotten. Not forgiven, just forgotten. Compartmentalizing is one of my most useful life skills, which made it easy to take the conversation with Erika only an hour before and put it in its little box to be packed away in a dusty shelf in my mind's attic.

Make the best of it. Do not let her take this experience from you. Do not waste one day hating her or what has happened. You are in Scotland. See all the beautiful things.

So, I did. We walked up and down rocky paths, and she seemed genuinely concerned when I lost my footing again and slid down the cliff toward the water.

Let it go. This is breathtaking.

It was easy to just clear my mind and follow her down

winding paths and over moss covered rocks, getting lost in the physicality of the hike. Then we found the stone ruins of the Hermitage and the waterfall. The observation deck provided the most beautiful place to take photos, and so I did. Briefly, I considered how much I would hate my life if I dropped my new iPhone over the edge into the rushing water, mostly because I would lose all my photos and videos of Scotland.

The raw power of the rushing water was awesome. While feeling the mist on our faces, I couldn't get past the fact it was stunningly beautiful. I closed my eyes.

I am grateful we are here together now, instead of being alone and stuck with the car in Pitlochry, freaking out about how to return it. This is amazing.

I loved the Hermitage, and it seemed to heal both our spirits being there. After we completed the hike, we walked back to the car and started driving to Glasgow.

"Let's return the car early," I suggested. "We'll save some money, and we can use the train and buses to get around for the rest of the trip."

For some reason, she agreed. We had a great day at the Hermitage, but I was unsure what Erika was capable of at that point. My main goal was to return the car and get out from under any obligation we had to each other in case there was another blow up.

"That sounds good. Glasgow is beautiful, and I haven't spent much time there," she said.

We drove for an hour, and I was surprised to see Stirling Castle again from the highway. It was my biggest regret of the trip. I had let her talk me out of it because I was concerned about her finances. We saw the backside of it from the road, and I was filled with longing and regret. The sun was setting, hitting the castle so that it glowed in amber light.

I won't ever get another chance to see that. I should have stood up to her.

Half an hour later, we pulled into Arnold Clarke and sat in the office to return the car. It was taking an abnormally long time. Erika was munching on shortbread and drinking their bad coffee in reception. Finally, the attendant called her over. "There seems to be some damage to the car."

"What? There is no damage. Show me. That's impossible!" She was outraged and strode out to the parking lot with the attendant. I followed along.

The attendant pointed out the dent on the rim and the scratches on the bumper and showed us the report that indicated there was nothing on it when it was released to us.

"She didn't go over the car with us. She just gave us the keys. That damage had to have been there from the previous rental!" Erika was getting angrier and pacing. "This is bullshit. I have never had an issue like this. It's normal wear and tear. I'm so fucking mad I can't even speak right now."

She was getting louder and pacing more and more. I was trying to quiet my mind and figure out what that was going to mean to my credit card.

"Can we put the car in her name?" she asked, pointing at me. "I mean, I booked it, but she's the one paying for it."

I was stunned at this selfish request. Even after all that had happened, her selfishness still shocked me.

"No, ma'am, we cannot change the name on a rental contract after the fact."

Erika was filling the room with tension.

"Why don't you go outside and let me talk to her?" I suggested, knowing I had to remove Erika from the equation if I was going to get anywhere with the lady behind the desk.

She stormed outside.

I sat down at the desk.

"According to our contract, we have the right to charge

your credit card 1000 pounds for damages. Since it's Sunday, we will send it to our body shop on Monday, get an estimate, and adjust it accordingly."

1000 pounds. That is $1300 American dollars. Puke.

My hand was in my wallet, clutching my credit card, and I was nearly ready to hand it over, thinking I was royally fucked. Normally, I would have, but then I stopped for a second.

"What happens if I refuse to pay it?" I asked with my newfound life skill called courage.

"Then, you are banned for life."

"Banned from what?" I asked.

"Erika Becker will not be able to rent a car ever again from any Arnold Clarke office worldwide."

Interesting. Hmm. I think I can live with that.

I smiled, happy for the calm, rational decision making I was finally learning to do here.

"Okay, then. I think I am going to refuse. You can get the estimate, and then once we know what the real damages are, we will find a way to settle up."

I kept my card in my wallet and walked out of there calmly and feeling capable and strong.

"What happened?" she asked eagerly, running toward me for a status update.

"Well, you can pay the damages or be banned for life from renting a car from Arnold Clarke."

"But I come here all the time."

"They are going to send the report to your email, and you can figure out whether it's worth it or not."

"I'll just use a different rental company then," she said, finding a loophole.

"Yes, you certainly can do that," I agreed.

We walked to the train, calmly and quietly. I felt ten feet tall.

"Wow, I was losing it back there. You were really calm. Thanks for that."

I nodded and smiled to myself. Yes. I was. That was a new one for me, too, and I was proud I was able to keep it together. *And* as a result, I didn't have an extra thousand pounds charged on my credit card.

FORTY-ONE

We got to our Airbnb in Glasgow, and it was in the thick of things—a short walk to the train in the middle of a very walkable city. Two more nights, and then we would fly to Dublin, and I would start the journey home. I was ready.

I pawned Erika off to two lovely young college students that shared our Airbnb. They entertained us with oddly hilarious, yet dramatic stories of their recent visit to Poland. They flitted in and out of our shared hallway, curling their hair and getting ready for a night out on the town, teasing each other with their melodic accents. They were so lively and fun to watch, and Erika walked right in their room, making herself at home. The girls were too sweet to refuse her invitation to tag along for the evening. She was desperate to go to the pubs, and I really wanted to stay in and read and relax.

I left the flat and walked out to the courtyard, trying to keep the peace with Erika, who was apparently on edge from listening to my phone calls back home. I will never understand how that was annoying and obnoxious, but she said it was, and I was trying to placate her.

I called Ryan.

"I can't believe you are still traveling with her," he said.

"The car has been returned, and she's going out tonight while I am staying in. Honestly, I was afraid to be alone in a strange country, and she has a UK sim card and can navigate with it. I don't even know where to begin to get one. I was afraid I couldn't figure it out, that I would be lost in the United Kingdom."

"Just download Google maps for where you are offline. You won't need to have Wi-Fi or an internet connection then. It will work without it."

"How does that even work?" I marveled at the magic that is technology, which always seemed like a foreign language to me. Luckily, Ryan was fluent.

"I'll send you a link with directions."

He was the king of sending links, and I secretly loved that about him. His deliberate way of approaching everything like a problem that needed to be solved was in sharp contrast to my reactionary way of living. He was always looking for ways to make my life easier, and he had really stepped up for me, taking care of everything back home, including my daughter, to make this trip possible for me.

I called both my kids. It was Mother's Day, and I just wanted to hear their voices.

"Hey, Mom." It was nice to hear my son's voice while being so far away.

"What have you been up to?" I asked.

"We went to Omaha for the day, just hanging out with friends."

"Have you been getting my pictures?"

"Yes. Wow."

"It's the most beautiful place I have ever been to. You'd love it. I can see why you want to live in Ireland."

We chatted a bit more about the trip. I promised to get him a souvenir from Ireland when I was in Dublin, and then we hung up. Our relationship had been so volatile that having a normal conversation on Mother's Day just made me ache for what could have been.

I wished we'd had the last three years together. I wished I had been around him every day to see him grow. I wished things hadn't been as crazy as they were. I wished I didn't parent from fear. I wished his dad wasn't an alcoholic so he didn't already have one strike against him.

I called my daughter then, and we chatted about school and what was happening. I was grateful that Megan was making her feel like part of her family. It was a relief that she was safe and okay.

"I miss my mommy," she said, and I could tell she really did.

"I miss you, too, honey. I'll be home soon. Love you."

I walked back up to the flat and took a bath in the biggest tub I have ever been in to date. It was even more strange that it was in a bathroom in Scotland, the country with the tiniest sinks and showers I have ever seen. I wrote for a while and then got lost in my book. For me, it was a perfect, quiet night of rest.

The trip was winding down. I was heading home in a few days, and for the most part, I had gotten what I wanted from this trip, but there was one thing that I deeply regretted.

I'd love to come back here with Ryan, but it is such a huge world. I wanted to see all of it, though, so the chances were small that we would return. My only regret was never going inside Stirling Castle.

I Googled it, finding it was only a forty-five-minute train ride from Glasgow and then a long walk up the hill. I could do that. I could get on a train. I could find my way to the castle. I could go without her.

I could. I could do it.

The next morning, Erika said, "It wasn't even fun. The music was so loud, they were shouting to hear each other. I felt so old." She changed gears quickly. "We *are* going out tonight," she demanded. "It's our last night in Scotland. Let's find a place with live music and go."

I reluctantly agreed and let her pick the place.

She settled on the Ben Nevis. Our plan was to take the bus there and then get back home on the last bus. She was a great navigator, confident in her ability to get us anywhere we needed to go. It was a strength of hers that I admired and knew I needed to cultivate more in myself.

The Ben Nevis was in the thick of downtown, nestled on a corner. It was a classic Scottish pub, with faded golden letters and dark paneling. It was a pretty bar and very tiny. We arrived about fifteen minutes before the music started, and it was already starting to fill up. Nearly standing room only, we were lucky to be able to snag the last chair at the bar. The "band" was three or four people who showed up with drums and guitars and fiddles and sat at the booths at the far end. An adorable, dark-haired violinist worked the crowd, asking for requests. When she got to us, we asked for the most cliché violin song of all, the theme for the *Game of Thrones*, and she nailed it. The pub was filling up after an intense game that literally had people shouting in the streets and drunk in the middle of the day. The hometown team had won, and everyone was celebrating.

It was standing room only in the bar, and I was grateful we had claimed a seat near the music. Erika was lost in the crowd, talking to people, I am sure. Sometimes I'd catch glimpses of her.

I heard him before I saw him. Stuart, looking like the son

of Gerard Butler, one of the finest genetic specimens ever produced in Scotland. A life of the party kind of guy, he worked the crowd, laughing and hugging people, and then landed next to me at the bar. He smiled and winked, and his brother was behind him, looking the polar opposite. Blond and thicker, he must have been the product of their mother's tryst with the mailman.

The big win or the many drinks consumed during the match—I couldn't tell which—had made everyone more jovial, and he struck up a conversation with me at the bar. His accent was thick, so I had to really focus to understand him.

"Hey, lass, you know there's only two types of girls in the world, don't ye?'

"Really?" I said, taking his bait. "What are they?"

"Girls who like to be choked and girls that don't know it yet."

Then he and his brother collapsed into a fit of laughter and smiles.

"What are ye drinkin'?"

"A cider."

He deftly signaled the bartender and ordered us all another round.

"Thank you," I said.

"What's brought you to Scotland?"

"Just exploring the country. It's so incredibly beautiful. You are so spoiled."

"Ah, yes, we are, and most people who were born and raised here have never taken the time to explore it."

"Where do Scots go on vacation?"

He threw his head back and laughed. "We go to Abu Dabi. It's so cold here, it's the best place to go to warm up."

That surprised me because it seemed so far away. But

then I remembered how far away I was, and a pang of homesickness for my kids and Ryan hit.

"Where've ye been?"

I rattled off all the towns and places I could remember. There were so many.

"That's impressive. I wager that most of the people in here haven't seen half of what you have," he said seriously.

"It's so lovely. I have never been to a more magnificent place."

Erika appeared, and I introduced Stuart and his brother to her. Stuart hit her with his same line, and she laughed. Then the music cued up, and I turned to watch them. Sitting in the booth, the dark-haired violinist pulled on her bow, back and forth, swaying in the seat. Next to her was a boyish man, not more than twenty, who was strumming on a guitar. Then there was a white-haired man on percussion, using a brush to gently tap the drum. It was lighthearted and festive and added to the cider. It was a warm, fun night that was going to be a great way to say goodbye to a country that was so incredibly sublime.

The band stopped for a break, and people mingled and talked. More drinks were thrust in my hand, and I learned that Stuart and his brother were entrepreneurs with a life-changing presentation similar to *Shark Tank* coming up the following week.

His brother was smarter and quieter.

"This one is my baby brother, and I love him more than anything." He wrapped his arm affectionately around his brother, pulling him in for a hug, and they swayed a little.

"I've always taken care o' him. Family is *the* most important thing."

The product was some kind of revolutionary design of a whiskey bottle that would be huge in the production of the most concentrated whiskey ever produced. He was the science, and Stuart was the salesman.

The band started up again, and this time the man on the drums pulled out a box of Tic Tacs and shook them gently in tune to the music. It was so unconventional and unique, I had to record it.

I was pretty buzzed when the bar was closing and looked at my phone in a panic. The last bus had already come and gone. We were miles from our Airbnb, and I had no idea how we were going to get back there.

I found Erika, and we started walking to the door amidst a throng of drunken humanity.

Outside at last, Stuart and his brother hailed a taxi. His brother sat in the front with the driver, and he waved us in. We all jumped into the back of the car, the effects of the cider in full force. Everything was a tipsy golden color, and I felt warm.

I leaned forward and gave his brother the address of our flat.

"Don't worry, lass, we'll get ye home."

"Thank you." I settled back into the back seat and closed my eyes, and then I felt a hand on my thigh. My eyes snapped open, and I looked at Stuart. When he winked at me, it felt wrong. I loved having a hand on my thigh, but it was attached to the wrong man. My guy was home with my daughter, and I missed him so much. Panicked, I thought the best solution was distance, so I quickly changed spots with Erika, who slid in next to him. She leaned in, and they started kissing, which shocked me. Then Stuart put his hand on her throat, and she reacted violently and head butted me in the car.

The cab pulled up to our hotel, the taxi driver waiting patiently. Erika was livid.

"What in the fuck were you doing?" she yelled. "That is not okay! You made me hit my friend."

Stuart matched her word for word. The Scottish are a lively cheeky bunch, and Erika had met her match.

"Let's just go." I pulled at her arm, but she was in the mood to teach him a lesson.

"You never put your hands on a woman like that." She was in his face. "You're sick! What kind of a sick fuck does that to a woman?"

They were like two rabid tiny dogs, jacked up, in each other's space, in each other's faces, yelling louder and louder. I am shocked the police weren't called. I went to the passenger window.

"Thank you for the ride. It was great to meet you both, and I hope the presentation goes well."

"Thanks, lass."

He was watching Erika and Stuart, shaking his head.

"I'll get her. You get Stuart," I said.

He laughed and said, "I'm used to that."

"Erika, let's go." I yanked her to the doorway.

"Piece of shit." She started to cry. "You should have heard the things he wanted to do to you." I was dragging her to the door, just wanting to crawl in bed.

"It's over. He's gone," I said, trying to calm her down.

"He wanted to hurt you and said that you liked it."

"I have no idea where he got that idea. We literally talked about travel and Scotland and where we've been. I'm drunk, you're drunk, they'd been drinking all day. Whatever happened, it is over, and we never have to see them again."

She was beside herself. Sobbing, mascara running down her cheeks, she got into bed and cried herself to sleep on top of the duvet cover. I had no idea what was happening. Did he hit a nerve or some other past memory? Was she feeling guilty that she kissed a man who wasn't her husband? I was so confused, but the room was spinning, so I texted Ryan and went to sleep, wishing I was snuggled up to my man-pie back home. I couldn't wait to see him again. I was ready to go home.

FORTY-TWO

Deep regrets the next morning. The hangover was brutal. Thank God there was an open shop two doors from our hotel, and I was able to grab a coffee and a hot bun with brie and bacon and some fruit.

Erika was moving slowly, too, and she was unnaturally quiet.

"That was a rough night," I confessed. "I'm *not* feeling great."

"Yeah, it was crazy. That guy was crazy," she said.

"I don't remember most of it," I lied, trying to let her save face.

"He was crazy, saying things like that. What kind of sick person likes stuff like that?"

"I think they were saying it for shock value."

"No, he was serious. He wanted to hurt you, and I couldn't let him do that to you."

Yes, kissing him was the best course of action in that situation.

In her mind, she was really saving me from a monster. It was almost laughable if she wasn't being so serious.

"It's over, let's just drop it," I said.

I closed my eyes, willing the Excedrin migraine to kick in, and steeled my reserves for a second.

"I'm going to Stirling Castle today. You can come if you want, but I'm going with or without you," I declared.

She sat up for a bit, looking at her phone.

"It's just forty-five minutes by train. I looked it up yesterday. I've never seen the inside of a real castle, and I doubt I'll get another chance."

My voice was firm and strong, and I liked the sound of this newly discovered independence.

"I'll come along," she said, so we got ready and called our next Airbnb host to pick up our luggage, and boarded the train for Stirling Castle.

The long, hilly walk up to the entrance of the castle chased away our hangovers, and we stopped frequently for coffee and pastries. We bought tickets for the tour, which was informative and funny in a proper Scottish way. We walked through the luxurious rooms, with the ornate ceiling carvings covered in copious amounts of gold leaf. We learned that the crest had unicorns, and there was a religious tie to the unicorns and their hidden meanings. It was fascinating. In some of the rooms, characters were dressed up in period clothing to demonstrate what life was like back in ancient times. Separate bedrooms for the king and queen. We heard about lavish parties held in the banquet and ballroom areas and watched other tourists snapping pictures of each other seated on the heavy hand-carved thrones.

The view from the castle was stunning and panoramic, overlooking a cemetery, and on the other side, the city spread out before us with tiny houses dotting the streets. It was a practically perfect day, and the weather was warm.

Then we walked down the hill toward the train station, where we boarded the train and headed to our final Airbnb so we could rest before heading to the airport in the morning.

We arrived there, exhausted and hungry. Stuck in a tiny spare room only two miles from the airport, we had walked through a pretty sketchy neighborhood to arrive there. Once again, Erika claimed the only side table in the room, and I just shook my head.

One more night.

We ordered takeout from a Chinese place I found on Trip Advisor, and it was a delicious departure from all the heavy food we had been eating. All the potatoes and fried fish. All the pot pies and ciders to wash them down. All the walking kept the weight from creeping up, but the food we'd been eating was very heavy.

I sat in bed, reading *The Outlander*. It was fun reading about the actual towns we had visited because now I could envision them in reality in my mind. We had actually walked on some of the same hallowed grounds described there.

We tried to go to sleep early, both exhausted from the long night before. The double bed we slept on was tight, and the pillows were flat and uncomfortable.

Erika whined, "Move over. You're hogging the whole bed."

I rolled my eyes. I was literally touching the wall with my knees *and* my feet. I moved over a few inches to satisfy her need for more room, feeling pinned between her and the wall. I closed my eyes and fell asleep, knowing this would be over soon and that I would never have to share a bed with her ever again. In the morning, we were flying to Dublin, and the day after that, we were flying home.

FORTY-THREE

One day in Dublin. It wasn't enough. Someday I'd love to go to Ireland and really see that country. Someday, I will.

Our plane landed in the morning, and I bought us bus passes. More expenses on my credit card. It was really racking up and was one of the reasons I kept a little more tight-lipped with Erika about my feelings during our trip. I had to be diplomatic in the words I chose during our confrontation in Pitlochry, knowing that if I burned all the bridges, I'd never get it back. And I *needed* her to pay me back. All the Airbnbs, bus and train tickets, the rental car, the airplane tickets. She owed me a lot of money.

The bus passes allowed us to travel the city on any bus for a 48-hour period. This turned out to be the perfect mode of transportation for our short stay in Ireland, but I was travel-weary and homesick, and for the most part, Ireland was wasted on me.

We were trying to find our last Airbnb so we could drop off our luggage and then have the day to explore the city.

Struggling to find a strong enough signal, we stopped at a pub, and Erika ducked inside to use the Wi-Fi.

A few minutes later, she emerged with a sweet, dark-haired, middle-aged Irishman.

"I'll take ye there," he offered.

"Really? Oh my gosh," I said. "That would be amazing."

"We're not far."

He picked up our luggage and threw it inside his car, chatting with us the entire time.

A few minutes and a few wrong turns later, we arrived at Tony's house, but sweet Tony was out driving around looking for two American girls dragging luggage behind them. The Irish are some of the sweetest, most giving, and generous people I have ever met. They entertain you with jokes and stories. The Scots are funny and generous story-tellers as well, but they have thicker skin and an independent, free-thinking streak that seems to temper their sweetness.

We dropped off the luggage, and after Tony gave us comprehensive directions on how to get to the city, complete with three different bus routes and the best place to eat lunch, we struck out to have our day in Dublin.

"I need to exchange my money," Erika said. The currency that had been pounds in the UK was now euros.

This again. Instantly annoyed, the frustration set in. We're here for *one* day, and having to waste it exchanging money was incredibly irritating.

"This is why you travel with a credit card," I couldn't resist saying with my newfound boldness. She ignored my stab, but it still felt good to say it.

We walked to *three* different cash exchange places until she gave up and accepted the rate and the fees.

"I'm getting hangry," I said, the frustration of the money

exchange process and hunger making me irritable. "There are a million options around here, so let's just pick one."

She had gotten a map from a tourist booth on the street, and we started walking toward the bar Tony recommended. I followed her, and unfortunately, we got stuck behind an entire class of school children that were dawdling down the sidewalks as if they had all the time in the world.

We passed donut bakeries and gelato vendors. Restaurants and pubs with people eating drool-inducing food on the patios. Each step made me crankier and more irritated.

"Can't we just pick one?" I whined. "Does it have to be the one he recommended?"

"Yes, stop bitching. We're almost there," she shot back.

Finally, we arrived at a non-descript black shop front. It was deceivingly small, judging from the exterior, but inside, Porterhouse Central Bar was quintessentially Irish, with the longest bar spanning the entire width of the restaurant. Chalkboards above the bar detailed the craft brew options of the day. After a minute, my eyes adjusted to the dark paneling covering every surface inside and small green shades casting cones of light on the bar. We settled into a high-top table, the cracked leather seats comfy yet slightly sticky, then placed our order with the waitress. Ordering only soup, Erika started eating in front of me, and I nearly salivated watching her. I imagine I looked like my dog does when I eat peanut butter in front of her without so much as an offer to lick a finger. At long last, my steak sandwich arrived, and I dug into it ferociously. Pushing my fries to the side to make room, I pulled a bottle from the caddy of condiments on the table. Ballymaloe Original Relish. It looked like ketchup but tasted like so much more. As I write these words now, my mouth is watering, knowing I will not get to experience it again until I drag Ryan to Ireland with me. I couldn't stop eating it, using my fries as a vehicle to shovel copious amounts of this sauce into my mouth. I am pretty sure that there is the finest amount of crack cocaine in the ingredients because it was that good.

Finally full, my irritation lessened. "So, what do you want to do?" I asked.

"Let's find the Temple Bar. It's the most iconic bar in all of Dublin."

We walked and walked and finally, tucked between buildings on the corner, was the Temple Bar. Painted red and packed to the rafters with tourists, flower baskets spilled gorgeous vines and colorful flowers from every window. It was charming, and I immediately understood why it was one of the most Instagrammed locations in Dublin.

"I need coffee," Erika announced.

Knowing that the quest to find sugar-free syrups in Ireland was about to begin, I felt the first urge to separate from her.

Changing her mind quickly, she said, "Let's find a rooftop bar instead."

That was the very *last* thing I wanted to do—drink all day and all night and then board an aircraft for nine hours with a hangover.

"We only have one day here. I'm sure we can find some live music, have some cider."

"I don't think I want to spend my last day doing that. But I don't want to hold you back either. If you want to do that, you should go," I explained.

"To a bar... by myself." She was hurt, pouring on the guilt.

"You make friends wherever you are," I said, pulling out this line of reasoning again, knowing she wouldn't be able to argue that point. I continued. "I think I just want to go sit in the park and relax. I don't want to drink again today, but you go and have fun."

The thought of escaping Erika sounded better and better.

A day of solitude away from her, in a city I didn't know, doing what *I* wanted to do. Big cities have never been my thing, but I wanted to enjoy my last day on my own terms. Real life was going to be resuming for me in a couple days, and I wanted this last day to myself. "Just meet me back at Tony's," I decided with more confidence than I felt.

I was a little unsure I could figure out how to get back there, but I wanted the freedom so badly I was willing to risk it. Besides, I had all day. Even if I got lost, all I had to do was reach out to Tony, who would give me three detailed routes on how to get back to his house, or most likely offer to fetch me at whatever location I landed at.

"Okay," she conceded, and then she turned and walked away from me. As I watched the crowd swallow her up, I felt free.

I walked down the streets packed with people, heading in the opposite direction of Erika. I stopped and watched street entertainers, some so great I felt terrible I didn't have any euros to tip them with. Men completely painted in gold paint that had become living statues. A full seven-piece band singing current hits with an Irish twist. Dogs trained to jump and retrieve almost anything, and a makeshift magic show with an entertainer so magnetic that he pulled people into his circle almost hypnotically. Other people tripped on the sidewalks, rubber-necking his act as they walked by.

I walked up and down alleys, mostly people watching and buying a few souvenirs to stuff into the only space I had left in my bag. I stopped for gelato and nibbled on the delicious treat with chunks of Ferro Roches inside it. Feeling like a child again, filled with joy in this sugary delight that was simple perfection. As I licked the cone, I walked and walked. In one alley, to my surprise and astonishment, I discovered hundreds of brightly colored umbrellas in all shapes and sizes suspended from wires. It was such a novel sight to see and so festive, I *had* to take pictures.

I finished my gelato and then found myself at the stone entrance of St. Stephen's Green. The weather that day was unseasonably warm for Ireland, and the park was packed with people. Some eating picnic lunches while pigeons dive-bombed for French fries, some laying on the grass, some sleeping in the sun, their hats covering their faces. I took off my hiking shoes and socks and wiggled my toes in the soft green grass. I picked a delicate white flower from the grass and marveled at its simple beauty, twirling it between my forefinger and thumb.

"When in Ireland," I said to myself, and I pulled out my iPad and wrote some words. I pulled out a sweatshirt and spread it out underneath me, laid back onto it, and closed my eyes. With a full belly, I relaxed, and the warm sun washed over my face, making me drowsy. I threaded my bag through my leg, knowing that if someone tried to steal it, I would immediately wake up. Then I put my earbuds in, and as Oprah's *Super Soul* podcast spooled into my ears, I let her voice lull me into sleep.

An hour later, I woke up, and it was starting to get a little cooler. I decided it was time to try to figure out how to get home. This was the part that made me anxious. I had followed Erika like an obedient little bunny all over Scotland, not having to navigate anything, not having to think for myself or take responsibility. That was how I normally navigated my life. I knew from Tony's description that I needed to get on bus 41. So, I walked and walked to all the bus stops, finally asking directions at a co-op that I ducked into to get a take away Caesar salad so I didn't have to leave the Airbnb for dinner when I got there.

I sat in line near the stop, with lines of people six deep all waiting for bus 41. Looking back, I maybe should have started back a little earlier since the workday was ending. The buses were running at peak capacity. Finally, a bus stopped, and I got on bus 41, not knowing that it would eventually get me there but it was actually going in the opposite direction of Tony's. I sat down in a seat near the window, and a middle-aged man sat next to me. Immediately, I tried to get on the free Wi-Fi and was panicking when it wouldn't connect. Knowing I had to download maps of the area I was in so I could use Google maps to navigate home without an internet connection was leveling up my anxiety.

It took me six years to feel comfortable enough to drive places in Des Moines without using GPS. I literally couldn't find my way out of a wet paper bag. My sense of direction was so wackadoodle, one might even use the word schizophrenic to describe it.

Why didn't I pay more attention when Tony drove us to the bus stop? Why didn't I dictate a note with street names or landmarks to help me if I got lost? 52%! Why didn't I fully charge my phone before leaving? What if I can't get home?

Finally, the maps downloaded, and my anxiety eased.

"Does this bus go to the Chalet?" I asked the man sitting next to me.

He laughed. "Eventually, yes. It's going to be a wee bit of a sit, though."

Wee bit. That little word made me smile.

Good, I can just sit here and relax until we get there.

He opened his book to read, and I looked out the window, watching Dublin race by me through the windows. People of all shapes and sizes got on and off, elderly women and small children, and blue-collar workers all just trying to get home. It was a virtual buffet of humanity pressed together in close quarters, holding on to whatever they could find to steady themselves as the bus lurched toward their destinations.

Finally, I saw the Chalet and got off the bus, thanking the

driver. I pulled out my phone and opened Google maps. I have a naturally skeptical personality, and even though Ryan assured me over and over I would be able to use it without Wi-Fi, I was still shocked to see that he was right. I entered Tony's address and pressed the little walking man then took off in the direction I thought it indicated. In true directionally challenged form, I actually went the wrong way, but I figured it out very quickly and course corrected.

I walked near a busy street with a roundabout, and then the relief flooded in when I saw a house that was familiar from when Tony dropped us off earlier. I kept walking, letting the Google gods lead me to Tony's. When I got to the door, he opened it up before I could even knock and handed me a couple bottles of cold water that I eagerly accepted, feeling triumphant. I made it back completely on my own.

"You made it! Brilliant! I was sticking around in case you got lost and needed a ride. But now that I see you are here safely, I am going out for the night. I'll be ready to take you to the bus stop at nine so you can catch your bus to the airport."

I thanked him profusely and downed the water.

Tony was easily the sweetest man and the best host we had encountered on the entire trip. He made his money in a fascinating way. I was an internet entrepreneur as well, so my ears perked up when he spoke about going to Thailand for a purchasing trip. He ran a store that sold mostly women's handbags and home décor, and he scoured the world for interesting and exclusive finds he could resell on his site. The Airbnb gig filled in some of the low months and gave him a constant stream of new people and experiences in his life. He was upbeat, happy, and a joy to be around, the epitome of every Irish person I encountered.

I took a long shower, ate my salad, and did some journaling and some reading, and then around ten p.m., Erika finally showed up.

"I had the best day. You'll never guess who I met at the pub." She launched into a story about Americans she met there who happened to be from Texas, and they stayed and listened to music all night, including several encores.

"I can't wait to see my husband," she said. "My horses and my kids."

Me either, sans the husband and horses. I was more than ready to go home.

Dorothy had it right. There truly is no place like home.

FORTY-FOUR

E rika's flight was before mine. It was fitting that she was compelled to buy one more coffee at the airport and, as a result, got held up at security. They patted her down and searched her bags to her dismay.

I went on ahead and got into the long line at customs, not waiting for her anymore. It snaked side to side in a huge room. I was desperate to get home, unwilling to wait even one second, knowing each step was getting me closer.

She finally caught up, irritated she had been searched, and talked her way to the spot directly behind me, cutting in front of several people in line.

Finally through customs, we stopped at a food court to grab something to eat. In the long line, I hemmed and hawed over whether or not to get a bottle of Ballymaloe's Original Relish. It was in a gift basket with a bunch of other useless things, so I decided to skip it, but man oh man, to this day, I regret making that decision. I got to see Stirling Castle, but I left the Ballymaloe's behind.

We ate that one last meal together, and as the minutes

ticked closer, I was getting more excited to get home. Finally, her flight boarding call came over the loudspeaker.

I turned toward her. "I'm grateful for you taking me all over this country. There were moments I would have never had, places I would have never seen, things I would have never done if it hadn't been for you," I told her, meaning every word. It had been a crazy trip, but being with her allowed me to see so much of Scotland I would have never seen otherwise, and I was indebted to her for that.

We hugged each other, and she waved and walked away, getting on her plane with a bottle of Jameson for her husband.

FORTY-FIVE

A week later, I sent Erika a Venmo payment request for her half of the expenses that were put on my credit card. Several days went by with no response from her.

Finally, I sent a text:

Me: Please repay me by June 1st.
Erika: I will do my best.
Me: You need to do better than that. I am not a
bank. Find another option, but you must pay me in
full.

Two days later, half of what she owed was paid through Venmo, with the message that she would pay the rest in a few days.

I was irritated but waited her out, and finally, a week later, another payment came through for most of the balance. The payment was short $10 but came with the comment, Paid in Full.

At this point, it was the perfect ending to the most dysfunctional travel experience I had ever encountered. Of course, she wouldn't feel compelled to pay me the full amount. Of course, this is how it would end.

It was close enough for me. I unfriended her on social media. I blocked her on everything, and until that moment, the only other person I had ever blocked was Cal. I cut off all contact with her and have never spoken to her again.

A few months later, a mutual acquaintance sent me a screenshot of a post from Facebook that Erika made about her upcoming trip. She was taking a group of women to Scotland in 2020.

Scotland 2020 is booked!
14 days of HIKING in the mountains, all through the Highlands. This trip is my recompense for the last one! Woo HOO! I am so flipping excited. We will be hiking and wild camping through the West Highland Way. I am beyond excited. It's going to be amazing.

Recompense. Truly the most laughable term she could have used.

Holy shit. Here she goes again. I smiled at her audacity.

A little part of me wished I could be a fly on the wall of one of those tents. I love a good drama. Hope she doesn't run into any Canadians while camping. We all know how that turned out.

FORTY-SIX

The Skype ring jingled, and I picked up my call with Noah.

"I can see your strength returning. Your face is shining. It is so good." A soft, compassionate smile spread across his face.

I smiled back. For some reason, I yearned to make this man proud of my progress.

"As you get stronger, you can sit in fear with greater strength. You will not be ruled by it."

"I *do* feel stronger. I am writing more, nearly every day, and not wasting away on the couch."

"That is incredible progress. Your emotions used to be so heavy and fatiguing. Now you have more energy so you can create more. We are opening up your receptors and clearing pathways that can bring in resources."

He closed his eyes and exhaled loudly.

"You have been the brunt of so much anger. You were the voice of accountability and the voice of clarity, and it became hard for them to hear the truth. For Toby, for Liam, for Cal. You are not responsible for their anger. They do not get to take it out on you. They push their crap onto you to keep you in a victim state. It is deadly for you to be the brunt of that anger."

He continued. "These patterns will take everything and leave you in a place of helplessness and fear. Look to shift, but not to attach or unattach."

He was especially profound today.

"Don't show up. Even good words from you are showing up. They do not have the right to coerce you into this position of participating in this pattern, where they get to create fear and helplessness again. It leaves everyone in a weaker state."

He stopped for a second, his fingers at his temple again, breathing. "Simply send out a statement of strength to them. Don't give advice, don't judge, don't say you will get through it. It gives them something very difficult to respond to. If they try to pull you into the drama, don't feed into it by giving advice. Just say, 'I hope you find strength in that.'"

Genius. This man is a relational genius.

"They can't continue to make their terrible decisions and then push their anxiety off onto you. All of them rely on you, and it's not your responsibility to hold this all together. They are trying to use you as glue, but this glue isn't good glue. It will never allow them to live in the power of who they are. It will always allow them to be the screw ups, and the feelings you are battling with will continue."

He paused for nearly a full minute as I patiently waited.

"You are always trying to mend brokenness. Remove yourself from the role of the glue. There is not enough glue to go around, and they don't even *want* the glue. All it does is exhaust you and your resources. Shift out of it. Don't be the glue. Being the glue has postponed the inevitable, and it has stunted their growth."

This is so true. I can see the part I have played in these dynamics now and why it will never work. I need to stop being the glue. I took pride in being the glue. Let them be their own glue. It is not my responsibility to hold everyone together.

"It is okay to be in the scary and uncertain place for now, but to change this permanently, everything has to shift. If you don't want to continue the bad patterns and the weakening, you have to create the change, and all along the way is scary."

It was scary. Terrifying, really. Uncharted territory. Intentionally creating new patterns, when falling back into the old patterns is so easy.

"Crazy is out there, and people are full of that. People are looking for someone like you to dump their junk on, and you are allowing it. JUST SAY NO. The more nos you get to say right now, the better off you are. Say no to almost everything until you get to a place in your head that is healthy. It's too easy right now for those patterns to repeat and undo the work you are doing."

He smiled, and I waved goodbye. His words always cut through all the noise and reverberated with my soul. The truth has a way of doing that. I was still working to change patterns, and he had become my guide to a healthier place. My sessions with Noah always shifted me into a more positive state of being and a healthier mind.

FORTY-SEVEN

Six Months Later

Scotland changed me. It wasn't the trip I thought I was going to be taking, it wasn't the trip I was promised, but it ended up being the trip I needed. The world has opened up to me now in a way it never was before, and I am excited to explore more of it.

As middle-aged women, we are all yearning to pilgrimage to a place of peace within ourselves. Craving the time and the luxury to focus on ourselves for a moment when knee deep in the business of motherhood seems selfish. It is not. The choices we made as teenagers and young women may have set us up for success or failure as adults, and we are processing everything in a world that constantly demands from us—taking more and more, as much as we are willing to sacrifice until we are completely empty.

The circumstances of my life wore me down to a passive doormat. It's not something that happened overnight. It was the slow assault of years of pain. Cleaning up everyone else's messes, being the one people could count on, overextending myself mired in co-dependency. I wasted so much time, blind to the slow spread of disease that alcoholism becomes in relationships.

The thing is, you can't see it when you are in it. Day to day. It incrementally becomes worse, moment by moment. A healthy person looking at my life from the outside would have easily been able to identify the mess. They would roll their eyes that someone could be that stupid, that weak. *I* see it now, and *I* agree wholeheartedly. But when it is happening, the shock and the stress change your ability to see things as they truly are. You are simply surviving. Every ounce of your energy is focused on self-preservation, not self-exploration. You can't see the forest for the trees.

By the time I woke up, shortly after my mother died, I was in my forties and my kids were teenagers. It was the worst possible time to course correct, and yet I did. The house was on fire, I was finally fully aware, and I was desperate to do something. Then, to make matters worse, I parented from fear and guilt, and devastation followed. I didn't take the time I needed at first to heal myself and my kids. Instead, I looked for someone to love me, and damaged people always attract damaged people.

I was a martyr, and part of my identity was proud of that, the willingness to be selfless and give until it hurts. To be the glue. It was my badge of pride. All the challenges that came my way, all the things I survived became even more sick badges of honor, to the point that I truly believe the universe said, "Oh, you think you got this? Hold my beer." And she dumped even more craziness and pain into a life already chock full of it. I attracted misery just by being proud of my ability to overcome it.

I am quieter now. I'm still working on my need to be

needed, on my desire to fix things for others and to take on their problems as my own. I am learning to say no, to not react, to disengage from unhealthy people who try to rub their crazy off on me.

The universe, in its infinite wisdom, paired me with Erika. We were opposite in nearly every measurable way. There are things I see and appreciate about her to this day— her unwavering confidence, her sense of direction, her determination to climb every mountain. She owned who she was, and when I met her, I was still buying and selling myself short, far from owning myself.

In spite of our personality conflicts, she navigated us successfully on an incredible journey that I was too afraid to undertake on my own. I would have never seen the sights I got to see or experience the awe-inspiring beauty of Scotland without her. For this, I am forever grateful.

The events of our trip were truly a laboratory of the spirit. Maryanne Williamson was right. They forced me to grow up, to speak up, and to make my voice heard. They taught me that true strength can come from non-reaction, and to take a breath and stand back and assess the situation before getting caught up in the drama. While the breakthroughs I had there may seem underwhelming, they were significant for me and were the foundation of new thought patterns and behaviors that I have built on since my trip. Lasting change also happens incrementally. It's not an about face or a single moment where everything flips; it's a lot of small steps married together to create a new reality. The little victories that I fought hard for in Scotland were the beginning of the biggest breakthroughs of my adult life.

Many people have asked me why I stayed with Erika after the car was returned. Why didn't I just get on the first train and get the fuck out of there? It was a layered decision. There was definitely the financial aspect of the large amount of money she owed me, but also, the trip was winding down. It just made sense to finish what I'd started. I did begin to advocate for myself though, and my biggest victory was separating from her in Ireland, claiming my last day for myself and navigating my way home. Admittedly, these were baby steps, but for me, they were significant.

I went to Scotland, not knowing who I was anymore. I was empty, lost, and broken. I didn't need anyone else. Turns out, I just needed to trust myself. Scotland taught me that. I am no longer a passive doormat. I finally know how to set healthy boundaries. I speak my mind. I can identify co-dependent behaviors and stop them before they start. I am strong and capable and confident in my ability to always find my way home. I have forgiven myself for the abortion. I have forgiven myself for the mistakes I made trying to parent my son. I have forgiven my mom for abandoning me when I needed her most. I can only take responsibility for my own life now, and I am doing that.

The older I get, the more I see that nothing is black and white; there are shades of gray everywhere, in every circumstance. We are all individual people whose views and values are colored by our own experiences. That is why two people can be put in the exact same situation and yet have completely different perspectives on what happened. We all see the world through the lens of our own experiences. I'm sure, if you asked Erika about our trip, you would hear a completely different story. This story was mine, as true as I could tell it.

Who goes to Scotland for two weeks with a stranger they met over the internet?

I did.

And it changed my life.

REVIEW ON AMAZON
REVIEW ON GOOD READS
REVIEW ON BOOKBUB

ACKNOWLEDGMENTS

Many thanks to my editor, Kendra, who took this story and polished it into the jewel that you hold in your hands. I don't know how to properly use a comma for the life of me, but she always makes me look like I do.

I also want to thank Kristi. She read this memoir in its weakest state and said, "It's a beautiful story. You have a very authentic voice, and you have something to say in this piece. It is good, and it is worthwhile." This comment brought me to tears initially and, when I doubted myself, gave me the strength to finish. I am so grateful to have you in my life.

READ MORE BY THIS AUTHOR

Non-Fiction

Scotland with a Stranger: A Memoir

First You Then Him: A Former Trainwreck's Guide to Becoming and then Finding a Healthy Partner

Erotic Romance

Velvet Guild Collection 1

Velvet Guild Collection 2

Velvet Guild Collection 3

Velvet Guild Collection 4

By Blair Bryan

(Ninya's Contemporary Fiction Pen Name)

Back to Before

Better than Before

The Sweetest Day

The Funologist

When Wren Came Out

AnaStasia Lived Two Lives

ABOUT THE AUTHOR

I've always been a risk-taker, so at 44 I decided to write and publish my own books. It has been a roller coaster ride with a punishing learning curve, but if it were easy, everyone would do it. I write under the pen names of Ninya and Blair Bryan.

I love to travel and a trip to Scotland with a complete stranger was the inspiration for my memoir. I also seem to attract crazy experiences and people into my life like a magnet that gives me a never-ending supply of interesting storylines.

If you love a good dirty joke, a cup of coffee so strong you can chew it, and have killed more cats with your curiosity than you can count, I might be your soulmate.

Visit me online www.tealbutterflypress.com

Join my facebook reader group: https://www.facebook.com/groups/ninyons